Beyond Concepts

The
investigation
of who
you are
not.

by Esther Veltheim

PUBLISHED BY PARAMA

By John & Esther Veltheim
  Reiki: The Science, Metaphysics, and Philosophy
  The BodyTalk System™, by John Veltheim
  PUBLISHED BY PARAMA

First published in June 2000
by
PaRama LLC
5500 Bee Ridge Drive, #103
Sarasota, FL 34233, USA

ISBN 0-9645944-8-X

Printed in the USA

e-mail: parama@home.com
Web site: www.parama.com

Cover design by Lorin H. Sourbeck
Layout and editing by Colleen Clinton

Preface

The other day, in the humor section of a bookstore, I picked up a book on sex after fifty. When I opened this rather large volume, I laughed to find all the pages blank.

When the title for this book came to mind, it occurred to me that it lent itself to another book with empty pages. Clearly, books are collections of concepts and to entitle one *Beyond Concepts* is an obvious paradox. What this book is about is exactly that—paradox.

The human dilemma of looking for meaning has come about because the paradox of life isn't recognized. While you think in terms of this versus that, the mind is 'split.'

You cannot conceive of having anything unless its opposite is absent. You can't conceive of freedom unless limitations have disappeared. You can't imagine peace unless strife is first 'controlled.'

In acknowledging sacredness, you are simultaneously acknowledging the existence of the profane. Because all concepts are dependant on the existence of their contradiction, no concept is an absolute.

When the paradox of life is deeply understood, duality no longer poses a problem. Perhaps you think that the problems you have now are real. Problems appear to exist only because you experience life as a collection of negative and positive forces that need to be controlled. The only 'problem' is the need to control.

If you experience personal limitations it's because you are identified with concepts. You think you Are a body, a mind, and perhaps a spirit and a soul.

You weren't born with a mind full of concepts. Before they entered your mind, no limitation was experienced. There was simply awareness—pre-personalized awareness.

Your birth may have been a difficult one, and sickness or other traumas may have happened. Until you had thoughts about any of this, experiencing happened, minus any thoughts of avoiding.

You may have cried and struggled, but all actions happened spontaneously. No experience, and no action, was censored. Everything was experienced fully.

How does this compare to your present experience of life? Is the freedom of spontaneous actions only a rare and fleeting feeling for you? If this is the case, it's because you think in terms of control, limitation, and attainment.

There is only one reason for focusing on 'becoming better,' or 'more successful,' or 'more aware.' The reason is that you spend most of your life dwelling on what was, what is not, and what might be.

To think 'his is how it is,' is to hold a rigid belief that you consider an absolute truth. You probably have a whole host of such ideas. Even though you may have 'changed your mind' many times during your life, each new belief is considered true at the time.

This arsenal of ever-changing truths is testament to the fact that you can never be sure of any-thing. Despite this, the mind continues to latch onto first this, then that 'truth,' until it finds one it feels really comfortable with.

The beliefs that rarely change are ones that describe you, such as, 'I am a person,' 'I am female,' or 'I am male.' You might find it quite extraordinary if someone told you that none of these beliefs are true either.

This book is about the investigation of self as a concept, a multi-faceted 'thing.' One might best describe what you are about to read as a book on un-learning. It isn't an analysis of you 'the person,' because I am sure you have analyzed yourself quite enough already.

Rather, it is the progressive deconstruction of who you *think* you are. The 'me' you are identified with didn't exist when you were born. This is because you didn't have a single thought in your mind that described you.

Once the personal descriptions began, the 'me' idea was born. You are not this 'me' with all its facades and identities. Of course, simply expounding this will not cause you to think otherwise.

The only way you can discover—un-cover—your True identity is by exploring who you are NOT. Before you can see beyond the conceptual self, you have to dis-identify with it.

Before this can happen, all concepts have to fall away. This doesn't mean that the mind has to completely cease thinking. It means that the thoughts you have about yourself need to be scrutinized, until they are disproved.

Under the light of scrutiny, all concepts show themselves to be invalid, including the concept of you-the-person you *think* you are.

Enlightenment is just a concept among many. It is a description only, of what happens when light is shed on your misconception of self.

The following may serve to en-lighten 'you,' but no words will take you to the Truth. Who you really are, is non-conceptual, un-namable, and beyond understanding.

Before this Knowing can happen, all understandings have to fall away. The concepts contained in this book are mere signposts that point away from your present understandings of self. If you adopt them as truths they will be of no use to you at all.

Until now you may have been concerned only with your evolution. As long as you are focused on evolving you continue to add to your pseudo-identity. 'Now I am more spiritual,' 'now I am less materialistic,' etc.

While your identities fluctuate and distract you with efforting, you cannot Know the effortless Self.

This book has nothing to do with personal evolution. It is about involution. This in-turning of the mind, gradually focuses it away from the personalized self.

As this happens, the desire to 'be-come' other than you are is dispelled. All that remains is the desire to see beyond who you are NOT. When this involution is complete, the quest for intellectual understanding falls away.

By means of concepts, and the investigation of the conceptual self, these writings may serve to point you in the direction of

That which is beyond concepts.

"Out beyond ideas of wrongdoing and rightdoing, there is a field. I'll meet you there."

JALALUDDIN RUMI

Contents

Preface   3

I just want to be myself!   9

What is Satsang?   23

Meeting Ramesh   27

Satsang: Knowing Yourself   41

Satsang: Mind Games   55

When you understand you Know nothing   67

Circles of the Mind   75

Relationships   81

Satsang: Predetermination and Goals   93

Pain and Suffering   109

Depression and the need to control   117

Satsang: The Struggle for Peace   125

Awareness   137

Being Present   143

Being in the Now   151

Author's Note   157

The Levels of Enlightenment   159

Illusion, relativity, and enlightenment   177

Satsang: What is Enlightenment?   191

How do you know that you are?   219

"I just want to be myself!"

"I think I know what it feels like to be grown up.
It's when you feel how someone feels
who isn't you."

Fairy Tale: The True Story
Screenplay by Ernie Contreras

At birth there is simply awareness, minus any sense of limitation or restriction. In this pre-personalized awareness inherent personality traits already exist. Because the mind is free of judgments the natural disposition isn't censored in any way.

Until the mind begins rejecting experiences, *all* experiences are felt fully—whatever they may be. Minus the stress of the censoring mind, even physical struggle is underlain by peace.

This means that at birth your natural disposition, your body, and your mind are peaceful and stress-free. This describes your essential, nature—that which is natural to you.

When the mind learns to judge, actions begin being censored. Then both the mind and body experience tension. Learned behavior patterns are superimposed upon your natural disposition and the false, unnatural personality begins forming.

At this stage, pre-personalized awareness has been personalized. This is when you begin identifying with the body, the mind, actions and roles. This collection of identities is then summed up in the word 'me.'

Clearly it isn't possible to go through life without thinking. Neither is it possible to eradicate all the beliefs you have. However, the beliefs that caused the false personality to be superimposed upon natural characteristics are of no benefit to you.

Before you learned to describe yourself as "I Am some-one," "I Am this," "I Am that," there was awareness only of being. All

9

the descriptions that have been added to this sense of being now serve only to give you a sense of limitation.

Although these accumulated identities are constantly changing you think of them as important. You need to look a certain way. You need to act a certain way. You need to think a certain way. If you don't, it means you are a misfit or will be ostracized and feel separate and alone.

Whether you rebel or conform to the dictates of society and 'others' your actions are unnatural. Modification of them is considered necessary because you need others to respond to you in a particular way.

The neediness for others to see you in a certain light is the existential dilemma. You are living life behind a set of facades. These 'fronts' are testament to the beliefs you have about yourself, "I Am not good enough as I Am." "I need to be-come like this or like that."

The desire to become other than you Are keeps you goal-oriented and the idea of 'having a purpose' or meaning for your life is all-important to you. Interestingly, the word purpose originates from the Latin word *intentus* meaning to struggle. As your essential nature is care-free and effortless, the belief that struggle is necessary is unnatural.

When people talk of being able to 'be themselves' it usually describes a time when they relax. The pressures of life are set aside, and they don't feel they need to act in any particular way to please anybody. They feel uninhibited and whatever feelings or actions happen they experience no need to suppress anything.

If you believe that you can only 'be yourself' at certain times, it signifies that you believe 'circumstances and other people limit me.' Another, more direct way, of saying this is 'being myself is a luxury.' This means that

your essential, peaceful nature has been forgotten. All that 'comes naturally' and effortlessly is now considered a luxury.

You may never have thought in these terms before. But, if you experience limitation and blame situations for it, it means you believe limitations are real.

You may be thinking that being childlike is impossible for a practically functioning adult. But I am not talking here about returning to the naïve innocence of the child. This would be impos-sible because, over your life, you have gained knowledge that cannot be erased completely.

What I am proposing is that the wisdom of innocence is possible for everyone. The capacity for childlike spontaneity and uninhibited self-expression need not be compromised because of anything you have learned.

Right now, if limitation is considered real, it has nothing to do with external factors. Rigid beliefs are what cause this *seeming* limitation. You probably think most of your opinions are valid and important, but in the next pages you will discover just how destructive and illogical your thinking has been up until this point.

The following descriptions are taken from lists compiled by students in my Breakthrough workshops.

1) When I am being myself I feel:
peaceful, open, uninhibited, spontaneous, centered,
non-judgmental, trusting, present, vital,
non-attached, carefree, honest

If you read this list through you might say it describes the 'perfect' person. It may even seem to describe the 'enlightened person.' This is because perfection is an ideal which, like all ide-als, is limited by the belief in 'good' versus 'bad.' *Understand that what we have listed are* not *descriptions of a person, but descriptions of a way of being.*

The word perfection, when attributed to the sage, does not denote the absence of what are considered negative qualities. The sage rejects absolutely no aspect of expression because he is not identified with roles, the mind, or the body.

Via the body of the sage the Knowing 'happens' that all ac-tions are spontaneous and impersonal—they happen despite 'him.' This means there is no experience of guilt and no sense of re-stricting any action.

Recognize that un-censored self-expression contains all fac-ets of the natural temperament. There is no self-judgment and no expectation of being judged. From this perspective, 'perfection' describes balance and impartiality.

You have probably never considered the uninhibited expression of negative traits to be a mark of perfection. But, the perfection we are talking about here signifies 'that which is natural.'

Each time you are 'being yourself,' you have a glimpse of your natural, uncensored nature. To feel you can be yourself with someone means 'letting it all hang out.' You feel you can act grumpy, silly, irreverent, and nothing is held back. This is why seeming 'negative' qualities—the ones you 'normally' censor— must also have a place on our first list.

anger, grief, moodiness, apathy, stubbornness, impatience
(feel free to add to these lists)

Until now your entire focus has been upon the unnatural 'you,' which *Is* imperfect—so you haven't been wrong there. The 'you' you are identified with is not only imperfect, but it is un-real because it is NOT YOU. It is a collection of acquired and contrived images you have of self. This false 'you' has been superimposed on who you Really are.

The false you is something you are used to thinking of as real. However, the fact that you talk of 'NOT being myself' means you are not fully unaware of this misperception--that is the good news.

Now, let's list some of the feelings you have when you are 'not being yourself.'

2) When I am not being myself I feel:
closed, inhibited, scattered, judgmental (of self and others),
rigid, stressed, involved, needy, guilty, limited, false, dishonest,
two-faced, angry, distressed, unlovable, false-pride, ashamed
(and the list goes on)

It's pretty obvious that this list is in total contradiction to the first list. The first list describes what comes naturally to you. The second list describes an unnatural way of being.

People often tell me that they are so used to putting up facades they no longer know who they really are. The fact that they are able, if with difficulty, to make the first list at all tells you that they are not totally unaware of what comes naturally.

The following chapters are an investigation of who you are NOT. This is why I begin here with this simple exercise. It helps you already gain a clearer perspective on the dynamics of how and why you act the way you do.

Clearly you cannot Be two selves, or have many so-called selves—even if this is your present experience. If you relate to the second list it means that your mind is 'split' between who you *think* you are and who you think you *need* to be-come.

Now—be honest—how much of your *entire* life have you spent being yourself and what percentage of it have you spent not being yourself? I have yet to have anyone in a class who can honestly say they have been themselves more than 10 percent of their life. Most agree that this is an optimistic percentage and the very honest ones say they doubt 2 percent of their life has been spent being that way.

We'll stick here with the 10 percent—so as not to depress you totally. This percentage signifies that you have spent 90 percent of your life not being yourself!

Now let's look at the reasons people give for spending most of their lives acting stressed, inhibited and guilty.

I cannot be myself because:
I need to be responsible.
People will think I don't care.
Society dictates that I should act a certain way.

I need to be responsible: This idea reflects the belief that spontaneity and lack of inhibition lead to irresponsible actions. Again, this is when rebelliousness is mistaken for spontaneity.

If you feel at peace, centered, and present, you know all too well that actions are also centered. Of course, you may not act how 'others' deem you *should*, but at least you are acting honestly—from your center. When you feel peaceful and uninhibited it also doesn't mean you are likely to act in ways that are harmful to others. When you feel peaceful you don't feel the need to change anything in an aggressive way.

One woman I recall told me, "But I still need to feed my

children and go to work." Why on earth would you stop feeding your children and stop earning a living because you feel peaceful and open? When a person is in this state they usually act very practically. The only difference is that practical day-to-day living doesn't elicit stress.

You see, there is a big difference between the shoulds you do that are unnecessary and practical living requirements such as work and raising a family.

People will think I don't care: At one time or another you have probably experienced the feeling of being carefree. If you had to go to work or help a friend in trouble would you have avoided doing these things? More likely than not, you would have undertaken these tasks with more focus, energy and efficiency than usual. This is because you were free of worry and concern.

The caring that is meant in this second reason has nothing to do with the heart. It has everything to do with the mind and worry. It isn't a matter of 'not being yourself' because you are worried about others' feelings either. It is because you are worried about how they will judge you.

Another point to mention is that when you put up facades, or a 'front,' you are showing others a dishonest, false persona. Would you say that this describes caring?

Society dictates that I should act a certain way: Again, this reason for not being yourself has nothing to do with your fear of offending society. It has everything to do with your fear of being judged in the eyes of others.

Why you spend 90 something percent of your life not "being yourself" is because you are fearful. The fear is that you will not measure up in the eyes of others. The fear is that you will not be able to control others' actions towards you. The fear is that you will be ostracized and feel lonely and separate. The fear is that you are not good enough as you are.

This last fear is the motivating force that keeps you focused on adding to all the facades. The need for purpose, control and validation is rooted in one little word—GUILT. And this guilt has come about because you are identified with being some-one who is lacking.

Maybe by now you have realized the illogicality of all this. As you have spent most of your life driven by the 'split,' illogical mind, I will spell it out for you, just to be sure you've 'got' it.

You wouldn't be able to describe someone you don't know. Similarly you wouldn't be able to come up with the first or second list unless these 'selves' were your experience.

Anyone, whatever their background, acknowledges attributes we have listed to these two lists. This means that *everyone* intuits their natural, essential nature to be peaceful and spontaneous. Everyone intuits that the need to put up facades is unnatural.

Now, if you could choose between being with someone who demonstrated the qualities in the first list and someone who embodied the second list, who would you choose?

Everyone wants the same thing, yet everyone blames everyone else because they can't have it! And this crazy situation persists as long as you hold the belief "being myself is a luxury, dependent on circumstances." Ridiculous isn't it? This is a classic description of victim—and blame—consciousness.

Do you think you would be yearning to 'be yourself' if the self you described was lacking in any way? Interesting isn't it, that you have spent 90 percent of your life focused on 'being' someone you dislike and feel limited by? All the while you yearn to experience what you *know* underlies this persona. Go figure!

When I first met my husband, John Veltheim, we often found ourselves doing such things as going to a movie and coming out to find that neither of us had really wanted to see that particular one. Each had tried to accommodate what was thought to be the desire of the other and ended up with neither of us enjoying ourselves. This was clearly a matter of lack of communication, but it brought about the idea for an exercise we both found to be very helpful.

Whether you try this exercise alone or with a partner it can be quite a revelation. What we used to do was every few days sit down and tell each other all the unnecessary shoulds we had done. This did not include loving acts we enjoyed doing, but those we didn't really enjoy doing, but did because we thought the other required them of us.

This, in essence, is the root existential problem. People spend their lives victims of shoulds they choose to adhere to. It may seem that others impose these restrictions upon you, but your beliefs alone are the culprit! You may say that your parents taught you these beliefs, or society, but that is an easy way of passing the buck.

All parents and members of society are in the same boat. If you understand the craziness of this dilemma and that living from shoulds is the human dis-ease, then surely it is time to look for a cure. If you remain finger pointing saying, "But my husband needs to change before I can; my circumstances need to change before I can," then you are choosing to stay a victim.

Your present attitudes, wherever they stemmed from, are now your own. All the shoulds and should nots you adhere to are also your own. In other words, it doesn't matter where they came from, or why. The external world doesn't need to change-- it's all an inside job.

If you are particularly prone to judging and blaming, this will be a daunting proposition. How much easier it is to blame the reflection others are giving you of yourself. Recognize that
how you see the world and what you dislike and reject about
'others' is a direct reflection of that which you reject, avoid,
and dislike about yourself.

True responsibility is when you stop projecting your own seeming inadequacies on others. Only then do unnatural over-reactions to life cease. The natural tendency to respond to all experiences then resurfaces.

If the old motto "...better the devil you know..." no longer works for you and you have the courage to face change, then you have won the first battle. You are not about to learn the power of positive thinking, but to unlearn all the rigid beliefs and opinions that obscure your essential, peaceful nature from you.

The attitudes you have about life right now may cause you to feel cynical. This is fine, because it is those very attitudes that we will use as stepping stones along the way. All thoughts about 'this is how it is' are going to be put in question and investigated.

By venturing into unfamiliar territory you are going to feel vulnerable, because your habitual boundaries will be shaken and weakened. What has given these boundaries substance is your sense of personal identity. This identity is how and who you think you *should* be.

You may feel lost along the way and this is precisely the point of the journey. All the opinions you have about yourself are going to begin falling away. This means that 'you' are going to begin losing sight of who you *think* you are. This self-image is the only thing inhibiting you from experiencing That which is beyond concepts and beliefs.

You would not say "I want to meet so and so" if you did not know of his existence. Likewise, the words "I just want to be myself," only enter your mind because you know that self exists. This is the good news; you already know at a core level that you are not yearning to experience a figment of your imagination.

If, at a core level, you know that who you Really are is carefree and peaceful, who is it that is restricting this experience?

The essential nature of anything is unchangeable. Even if you melt an ice cube its essential nature, water, will still be water. A lump of gold when fashioned into a bracelet does not lose its essential nature, but is still gold.

Your essential nature is peaceful, uninhibited and spontaneous, and believing otherwise has not changed you in-essence. The only problem is that you do not believe this. Your disbelief makes all the difference between a life of struggle and one underlain by peace.

Perhaps you have arrived at a point in life where you can honestly say, "I know that deep down I *am* a special person," "I *am* a worthwhile person." This is a very good step in a direction toward self-acceptance. Unfortunately *any opinions about yourself, however positive they may seem, are—ultimately—a limitation.*

This is a sweeping statement, I know, and here is another one. *All positive affirmations are nothing more than temporary damage control.* This may sound ridiculous to you if you are feeling buoyed by a newly gained, positive sense of self. I in no way intend to devalue your arrival at this new stage of self-acceptance.

Having arrived thus far means that you have a new inner strength. This means that you are now ready and able to accept challenges that would have been impossible to face before.

People only feel the need to state that which they feel is in doubt or not obvious. For example, you would not go around telling yourself and others, "I have a nose in the middle of my face," would you? This would be ridiculous because you know this to be a fact that is evident to you and everyone else.

If you know beyond a shadow of a doubt that you are fine just the way you are you don't need to focus on such thoughts. You do not focus hard on your nose in order for it to stay in the middle of your face. But if you are balancing a spoon on the end of it you may well need to focus. That is because the spoon is not a natural appendage to your face. Similarly, your false persona is not natural to you. This is why it requires constant effort to keep it in place.

As an illustration, let us say that you get up in the morning facing the same problems as the day before. Life is chaotic, you are trying to get the children ready for school and have burned breakfast. Yet, inexplicably, you are surprised to find that you feel great. It's unlikely that you will now sit down and spend hours pondering why you feel so good. You simply enjoy it while it lasts. The only time you think about why you feel a certain way is when you don't feel good, or feel the need to suppress emotions.

Likewise, the only reason people universally question the meaning of their existence is because they are not happy as they are. If you are mystified as to *your* meaning of *your* existence and I give you a meaning, will it make your life any different? Will you feel more fulfilled? Will you feel less fulfilled if I tell you that you are here simply because you are here?

Do you feel special when you experience the qualities of the second list? I doubt it. Yet while you live from the perspective of the second list you are always aiming at specialness.

To describe qualities of who you are NOT is to describe the qualities of something that is un-real. How can you make something un-real special? Clearly you can't. This gives you a pretty good idea of why you might be experiencing life as a struggle.

Like Don Quixote you battle with the windmills of your mind. The 'inner demons' you struggle against are nothing more than an illusion. Yet you spend most of your life engaged in this losing battle.

You learned very young that certain aspects of your personality were unacceptable. This caused you to modify them, hide them, and battle against them. Yet if you look at nature, you'll see that both negative and positive qualities are present.

Animals aren't always gentle, but kill each other and even abandon their young. The weather isn't always 'perfect' because changes in climate are necessary. Plant life grows and then dies and replenishes the soil.

Similarly, your nature is multi-faceted and contains both positive and negative aspects. Having spent most of your life focusing on what is false about you, you have forgotten what is natural. You have mistaken the un-real for Reality and can't understand why it never meets your expectations.

You want only to express positive qualities. You want others only to see your 'good side.' You want only to experience positive qualities in yourself. All these wants point you away from what Is, toward what is not. All these wants belong to the false 'you' and keep you rejecting what Is, focusing on what should and might be. Simply put, this means that you are rejecting life, and you have spent most of your life rejecting it.

You weren't born with a mind full of expectations and needs-- and this absence was experienced as peaceful. Now expectations about how you *should* be are all that is standing in the way of re-experiencing this peace.

The first list we made describes qualities that you rarely experience. When you read them through they describe a seemingly 'special' way of being. Because this experience is one you only have glimpses of, you consider this way of being a luxury. Yet, everyone participating in the making of that list, whatever their background, comes up with similar words.

As everyone glimpses these 'special' qualities in-potential within themselves, it means they are common to everyone and, therefore, very ordinary. The desire for specialness is the greatest obstacle to Knowing who you Really are. This is because it keeps you focused on embellishing the false 'you.' It is not a matter of 'becoming special,' but of coming into your ordinariness.

If you are reading this book it may well be that you consider yourself a seeker. In this case the kind of specialness you seek is probably summed up in the much misunderstood word 'enlight-enment.'

The trouble is, it is the 'you' of the false facades that wants 'enlightenment.' What you need to understand is that enlightenment signifies the falling away of falseness.

If you aim at 'attaining' *anything* it means you are adding to your existing sets of masks and facades. If you are efforting, performing disciplines, or doing *anything* to 'attain,' the false persona is being strengthened.

If you relate to the first list it means you intuit spontaneity and peace to be your essential nature. Now ask yourself, "WHO? cares so much about becoming and achieving?"

All you need to 'become' is clear on who you are NOT. When this happens, what will be left is the Knowing of who you Really are.

Like a feather, touched
By the whim of Your breath,
I fly, I fall, I hang,
As if suspended
In that space
Between You and me.
The breath, the feather
Dancing in unison.
This strange
And constant dance,
Where You dance me
And I perform.
And then, with certainty
I know there is
No You, no me.
And in that space,
Between You and me,
I lose myself.
No thought, no word,
No understanding
Can come close,
To what is beyond them.

E.V.

What is Satsang?

Somewhere in one of his books, I recall Nisargadatta Maharaj responding to a visitor who referred to, 'being in satsang' with him. In his unique, endearlingly abrupt way, Maharaj answered, "That's just sprititual jargon!"

When I was first 'cornered' into talking to groups I was asked to 'give satsang.' Althoug the word is Sanskrit, it appears to be a familiar one to seekers, at least here in America.

At first I was hesitant to use an exotic, foreign word for the talks. I wanted it to be clear that the subject being covered was not airy-fairy, but very grounded.

The first satsang I gave was quite impromptu. My husband, John, came home one evening with a group of people. All of them had visited various gurus in India and America. When he talked to them about me during one of his seminars they asked if I would give them satsang. John agreed, in his usual spontaneous way, and so I sat down and, at first awkwardly, responded to their questions.

The awkwardness was in playing a role that was totally new to me. Until that day, I had been happy to 'stay in the closet,' as it were. I couldn't think of any good reason why, after a lifetime as a miserable seeker, I would now voluntarily hang out with more of them.

After that auspicious evening, I agreed to hold regular talks. Somehow, the word satsang stuck as a description of them. As quite a few of the following articles are in satsang format, the following is an interpretation of the word.

Traditionally, satsang means 'association with the wise.' This interpretation immediately gives weight to the misconception of

23

'the enlightened person' as some-one who is infinitely wise.

The meaning of 'wise,' within the context of satsang doesn't refer to wisdom as you think of it. The wisdom that is talked of here has nothing to do with accumulated knowledge in the general sense. The guru's, or Jnani's, wisdom is, paradoxically, the Knowing that no intellectual understanding contains any absolute truth.

The guru considers all actions and words as impersonal happenings. If you, on the other hand, still think of yourself as somebody, you consider all actions personal. The faulty perception of this identity is unnatural, and has lead to a life of guilt, pride and suffering. You avoid this, cling to that, and in general feel out of control of your life and self.

When this suffering becomes unbearable, you may 'become' what is called a seeker. That is, you consciously seek out answers to all your questions about "what is the meaning of life?" and "why am I here?" If the seeking becomes intense enough a teacher eventually appears.

Sometimes, this meeting is by chance and you may not even be aware that you are talking to a Jnani. Sometimes the meeting is in the setting of traditional satsang.

When such a meeting happens it is beneficial to understand that 'you' and the 'other' are not exchanging information. What is happening is that the impersonal Self is ready to commune with Self. Better put, Consciousness is at play within its-Self, and impersonal communing is taking place.

In your case, it may be that the Self is still obscured by the 'me' identity. Then you think in terms of 'me' and 'others,' and acknowledge a real difference between people.

The guru represents impersonal functioning. That is, no essential difference is seen between any two people from the Jnani's perspective.

If you think of the guru as different because of specialness, the mind risks desiring that specialness. Then you will listen to the guru with the mind, wanting to understand how to 'attain' what he has 'attained.'

You can only attain something you don't already have. In realizing the Self, the guru has not realized any-thing that was absent. All that has happened is that the 'me' idea has been recognized as the false self.

If the perception of specialness leads to awe of the guru, this can also lead to humility. This happens when awe transforms itself into what is called phala-bhakti. Phala-bhakti is the expression of love for the Divine. It is very different to the love between two people.

When love happens it is always spontaneously. It is not felt toward the guru, although this may be the interpretation, but toward the Divine. In such cases the unconditionality of this love serves to dispel the conditional 'me,' albeit perhaps only temporarily.

The most beneficial understanding of satsang is that it is an arena in which impersonal communing takes place. If you go to satsang with a mind full of personal agendas, unconditional listening will not happen. You will sit there in the capacity of a 'me' listening to the 'other,' and probably comparing your personal beliefs to the words you hear.

When the mind is open listening happens beyond agendas. Then it is not a matter of 'you' receiving information from another. There is simply listening happening and the words are more likely to bypass the mind and go straight to the heart.

In reading this book, a form of satsang will be taking place. Some of the concepts put forward may challenge your mind. Only if you read with your heart, not struggling to understand, can the words be of any use to you.

No words in this book are to be latched onto, or considered absolute truths. Their purpose is to dispel misconceptions only. If you adopt any words as truth you will simply add to the mind's rigid covering of the heart.

This book is the investigation of who you are NOT. The mind can never know your True nature, but it can recognize who you are not. If your investigation is intense and unwavering, only then can the Truth be known. This Knowing cannot happen with the mind, because it can only understand relative truths and concepts. Who you Really are is non-conceptual and beyond words. When the mind deeply acknowledges this it eventually gives up trying to understand. Only when the mental covering of the heart subsides can you discover—un-cover—the Truth within your own heart.

Within the following pages it is this relative process of 'subsidance' that is talked of. I have included quite some detail on my experience of this process. This is not so that you can better categorize or judge me, but so that you can put your own relative experience into a clearer context.

Meeting Ramesh

It was about eight years ago that I first discovered the teachings of Ramana Maharshi. Until then I had been more fascinated by psychology, Jungian, in particular. Philosophy sounded like a daunting word and the little I had read didn't touch me in any way. Clearly teachings only come to you when you are ready for them, so perhaps I was a late bloomer.

Thoughts about 'enlightenment' had never occurred to me. During my times in India I had absolutely no urge to seek out gurus. In fact, I had quite an aversion to the idea. From my limited perspective, it seemed that the followers of gurus were very dependant on them.

I had only ever thought in terms of knowing myself. I wanted to know why I 'ticked' the way I did. Although, even in my forties, friends still kidded me with, "What are you going to do when you grow up?" the idea of an ultimate purpose never entered my mind.

Oddly enough, it only recently occurred to me that I never felt I was lacking—or even needed—a purpose. I also never questioned the purpose of life—not even during my frequent bouts with depression.

During childhood I observed adults with 'a purpose' and they never struck me as happy. As hard as I tried, I couldn't figure out why unhappy adults thought they could give me a recipe for living. Perhaps the only purpose I ever felt driven by was the desire to understand myself.

As a child, I was happiest spending time alone in my secret hideaway in the nearby woods. As an adult, even though I traveled extensively, much of the time I journeyed alone.

When relationships happened they were usually a mixture of agony and ecstasy. It was obvious they made me look at those aspects of myself that, alone, I was able to avoid. Ultimately, they showed me who I was not, and this appeared to be their gift.

In 1989, when hit by neuro-toxic poisoning, my system went into overload. I had no short-term focus and was no longer able to function as a teacher, bodyworker—I lacked even the ability to read. My mind became incoherent and the carpet was pulled out from under my identity. Though I had long sought to understand myself, this was the first time I ever asked the question, "Who am I?"

A couple of years later, when Ramana's teachings of Self-enquiry came my way they made total sense. My reading capacity was still limited to a page a day because of the nerve damage, but the principles of his teachings required no lengthy reading.

About a year later, with some modicum of understanding under my belt, I came across the books of Ramesh Balsekar. His words hit me like a bolt of lightening. Immediately I called my husband, John, in England and blurted, "This is it, this is it. I've found someone who puts it into such clear words!"

When John returned from his lecture tour we began to read Ramesh together. Then, one-day I arrived home to a smiling John saying, "I've found him! He lives in Bombay, and here is a plane ticket. You are going to see him." This tells you everything about the man I married—he's a true gift.

My guru-phobia immediately kicked in and I insisted it was quite unnecessary to see Ramesh. "I have his books, why would I need to see him? I don't need a guru!" Then there I was, standing on a doorstep in front of Ramesh—a small, skinny gentleman with glowing eyes and a smile to melt the hardest heart.

To my horror I burst into tears. Within half an hour I found myself saying, "I can't understand it, I had such a strange idea about gurus. Now I feel as if I am totally in love with you and yet never need to see you again. I always had the impression that people who went to gurus were needy."

Ramesh smiled and said, "That is what true love is, empty of need." At the same time it was clear the overwhelming love I felt had nothing to do with the gentleman sitting in front of me.

As I had arrived in the rainy season, Ramesh had no visitors. He called it his 'slack period.' For nine days I would go every morning at ten to his apartment. For two hours beforehand, and during my entire time with him, I felt as if every atom of my body was vibrating at a hundred miles an hour. I was sure I was shaking all over, and yet there was no evidence of this.

Ramesh first asked me why I was there. "Well, my husband sent me," I muttered awkwardly. Then I found myself saying, "It seems to me that in front of other people I see aspects of my personality I like or don't like. In front of you, with the persona absent, I thought I might glimpse the Self. I understand that all I can do is surrender, and that 'I' cannot even do this. So, now what?"

When Ramesh began to talk I interrupted him with great urgency asking, "Do you teach in silence?" I knew this is how Ramana had taught much of the time and felt my mind would get in the way if words were offered to me.

Ramesh chuckled and said, "Well, usually I talk, but we can sit in silence if you prefer." So, there we sat and my discomfort and awkwardness became unbearable.

Ramesh laughed and began voicing the teachings, but much of the time we just chatted. He told me of his trip to America and asked me about my life. All the while my heart ached with an intensity I had never known. It is said that the guru's words are like an arrow in the heart. In this case they felt more like a hand-grenade. I was sure my heart was going to explode and that I would keel over and die.

For four mornings this continued. Tears pouring down my face much of the time while Ramesh chuckled and handed me Kleenex. What I remember most about him is the way he would shake his head and sigh, "Ah Esther, Esther, dear Esther." This reminded me of my mother, my grandmother, and the nuns at the convent school I went to as a child. They all used to tell me they had no time to pray for anyone else, they were so busy praying for me.

That fourth morning, I left Ramesh and set off for my hotel. There, in the midst of all the hustle and bustle of Bombay, I suddenly burst into uncontrollable laughter. For the rest of the day I cried and laughed and my heart, that had felt so constricted, seemed no longer to even be contained by my body.

The next day Ramesh asked me what had happened and when I related it to him he smiled and said, "Yes". Then I asked him, "Will my heart close again," and he said, "No, it never will."

When I telephoned John all I could keep on repeating, between spurts of laughter, was, "Nothing matters, absolutely nothing matters." John's response was, "It's happened, you are awake!" To which I assured him, "Nnah, don't be silly, that would never happen to me. And, anyway, even that doesn't matter any more."

Upon my return to the States the sense of apathy—not caring—grew. At first it was wonderful, but then the deepest, darkest depression of my life hit. All I could think was, "Ramesh was wrong, my heart is closing down."

At first it seemed as if everything mattered, but actually all that mattered was that nothing mattered.

In retrospect I now recognize that the 'me' who cared (worried) about life had all but disappeared. What was left were habit patterns that told me apathy was bad and that I *should* care.

The other habit pattern was just as deep. Since childhood I had understood that 'God' is everywhere and in everything. This made total sense to me and made me question why people judged each other.

How could anyone be essentially 'bad' or 'better' than anyone else. Unfortunately, I believed that the only person in whom 'God' did not dwell, was me. Not very logical, but then the mind quickly sets like Jello as we age.

During the second year of depression, despite a still limited capacity to focus, I began writing. My book (unpublished) was called *Who? Cares*.

Scrupulously, I investigated every rigid belief and every concept that came to mind. Each day I would sit on the deck with John, reading my latest chapter to him. What I could not understand was how such effortless clarity was there while I was still obviously 'asleep.' As long as writing was happening, however, there was no depression. That was incentive enough to continue.

After four hundred pages the writing stopped and the depression returned. At about that time we packed up our zoo of dogs and cats and moved to Florida. After five years living alone in the countryside, with John away traveling, the experience of a city was very strange.

Nothing much changed because I rarely went beyond my front door. However, I did resume teaching Reiki and Breakthrough courses. One weekend I was teaching at home and on the second day I lost all sense of my body. At one point I was so disoriented I had to excuse myself and lie down. My mind simply no longer functioned and I went into a strong altered state. At another point I found myself talking incoherently and simply having to sit silently. It was all very confusing.

Then, that night, pressure rose up into my head, making the top of it feel like a pressure cooker. I felt extremely dizzy and nauseous, and the pounding in my head was terrifying. I understood the experience to be the phenomenon of kundalini, which I had frequently had—but never to this degree.

The next day I sat listening to my friend Elaine, who was visiting us from England. Having read a little of my book she asked, "You don't care about anything anymore. Hasn't the 'me' disappeared?" It didn't take me a second to reply that, "Of course the 'me' is there. It's very much there. At least I think it is."

For the next few hours I continued muttering to myself, "Nah, the 'me' is definitely very much alive and well. Definitely!" I eventually realized that anything one has to keep on affirming indicates underlying doubt. With this I began investigating what it would mean if the 'me' were gone. Clearly it would mean there was no more involvement—'aha!'

With this understanding I sat down and spent all afternoon thinking about things that easily made me feel guilty. I thought about things in the future that easily set me worrying. As hard as I tried the mind didn't take the bait. Then I tried imagining the most horrifying scenarios of John dying in a terrible accident, and my dogs being killed.

With a very vivid imagination, it had always been easy to stimulate emotional changes in myself. But now the mind just wasn't engaging in any form of emotional involvement at all.

Getting desperate, I even imagined being in a foreign country where someone insisted I eat raw snails. You cannot image the lengths I went to, to find involvement; the very thing I had so long sought to free myself of.

Over the next days laughter just burst out of me. Over the following weeks there were several so-called 'peak experiences.' For a week there was simple bliss, sheer joy. It then was clear that much of the 'me' had disappeared, but I knew that such feelings of bliss and gratitude were being experienced by some-one. Clearly, these states were not 'it.' Something had happened, but some-one was enjoying the results.

I decided to pay no attention to the feelings, other than to enjoy them. Certainly I made no effort to hold onto them. This 'stage' I now understand, in retrospect, is what is termed '*buddhi*' in Vedantic philosophy. Buddhi basically means intellect and can happen throughout a lifetime in glimpses. At such times there is bliss and spontaneity of speech and action.

From a Vedantic standpoint, 'awakening' is broken into various stages. I had never really understood or related to these. When the experience of Buddhi happened, it was simply evident that it must not be latched onto.

Every case of so-called 'awakening' presents differently. It is determined by the nature expressed through the particular bodymind. Quite frequently people who enter the Buddhi stage fall into the trap of believing they have 'attained' enlightenment. They expect enlightenment to be blissful and they have every indication that they have achieved their goal.

Of course, if the Self is who you already Are, there is no-thing to be 'attained.' It is only the 'me' that desires enlightenment. If enlightenment in—and of—itself is the goal, it is usually because the person desiring it wants specialness.

When buddhi happens and the experience of it is owned, pride is the quickest way to make it disappear. This is because it is the 'me' that feels pride and ownership. Oftentimes one hears of students lamenting the 'disappearance' of the feelings they had after visiting their guru.

The ownership and desire to maintain those feelings is what has got in the way. The 'me' idea resurfaces in all its pride and glory. In this case, the bliss was recognized as an altered state, being experienced by some-one, and nothing more.

After a week or so, this perspective 'divorced' itself not only from the feelings, but also from the body. Depression arose again, but it was clear that 'I' was not depressed. It was clearly and simply that there was depression.

All manner of strange phenomena continued in the body and it was all observed from the perspective of the Witness (as it is often called). The sense was that there were parallel worlds—me and the body and other objects.

What was most surprising was that thoughts would arise and immediately be cut off. It was as if someone was channel surfing my mind, skipping from one thought to another with no involvement in any particular thought.

My stepdaughter, Anja, decided that if forced to explain me to her family, she would simply say I had Alzheimers. John declared that now I had really turned into the stereotypical blonde.

This was actually the 'easy stage,' because everything appeared to have a dream quality. Then one night thoughts of God began to surface.

When I had sat in front of Ramesh, love of the Divine had been so strong. Despite all my intellectual understandings, only then did it hit me that Self-realization meant that that love would have nowhere to be directed.

Images came to me of myself as a child, playing alone in the woods. I remembered my overwhelming joy in the knowing of God who was everywhere, in everything—if not in me.

Despite all my intellectual understandings, the belief in God and the love of worship now resurfaced. As surprising as it was to me, I experienced tremendous anguish at the idea that God and 'I' were not-two.

I suddenly found myself praying, using the words I had used all my childhood, "Whatever it takes, whatever it takes." I thought my heart would break, and in that moment the emptiness became 'more empty' than ever.

The next day I realized that the 'Witness' had disappeared. There remained only the strong sense 'I Am.' There was no longer the idea 'I Am this or that,' simply 'I Am.' Then depression arose again and this time it was not witnessed at a distance. There was no effort to suppress or reject anything. There was depression, but it didn't matter, even though my mind was still confused by it.

There was total conviction that 'I Am not this or that' and with that came the sense of limbo. Swinging in the wind, my mind turned in its usual frenetic circles trying to understand what was happening.

Then the sense 'I Am' turned into 'I Am NOT the Self.' The mind went crazy trying to figure this all out. There seemed to be no more involvement, but the 'Self' I had been seeking was also not evident. The mind understood this to mean that the seeker had, as yet, not fully disappeared.

Ever attentive, and with a very clear perspective on what was going on, John relegated me to an apartment by the ocean. "You need solitude," he counseled me. I couldn't understand why I would *need* distance from others.

Each time I would pack up and go off to my elegant hermitage I realized that the relative changes were a trauma to the body. With no 'me' to orient itself to, the body felt very disoriented much of the time. When I was around others there was a patient impatience because the relative process seemed to stop. As soon as I was alone, it continued.

People would ask me what I did 'in retreat' and were surprised when I told them I smoked cigars, watched TV, and played computer games. It is the idealistic stereotype of a meditating, vegetarian, disciplined human being that is so often the greatest obstacle to knowing Self. This is why the majority of 'those' who have 'awakened' had first to deeply live out what they most rejected about themselves. That had certainly been my 'path.'

While my body underwent fairly traumatic phenomena, the mind, too, had its process. It was not ready to give up its need to explain all this to itself. Eventually, by going to its limits and seeing its essential madness, it ceased questioning. Then the sense of Amness, or physical density subsided and all that remained was the sense that Consciousness, or Experiencing is All. And this is just words, which fall short of that which cannot be put into words.

Because it felt so natural, so ordinary, I still thought nothing had been realized. And, no-*thing* had been realized. With the total realization of who I was NOT, no-thing remained. As the 'me' had never been real, clearly nothing had *really* happened.

Despite prior intellectual understandings, I had expected 'awakening' to be a strong altered state. When the naturalness of it was understood I knew that the 'me' idea *had* been the altered state.

I remember Wendell, my main spiritual teacher, writing, "The disappearance of the 'me' is only ever known in retrospect." I also remember thinking, "No way. If I wake up one morning and Esther is gone I'll know it immediately and give such thanks!"

It is a misperception that when the false identity is recognized there is an immediate understanding of it. This seems to be the case in certain instances, but in this case there was a very delayed acknowledgment of it.

The subtlety of ones essential nature is a tremendous contrast to the density experienced when the 'me' is identified with. It is clear that nothing has Really happened to Me, but this doesn't mean that the relative experiencing stops. The objective world is experienced as before, but the Knowing is that no-thing Is as it *seems*.

Relativity (the objective world) is merely an appearance in Reality, When it is realized that relativity is NOT Reality, it's clear that nothing has *really* happened.

Relatively speaking, however, a great deal happens. The changes are dramatic, positive and even traumatic. Because the body is still experienced, so are any changes that happen to it. The difference is that no-one thinks of them as personal. However, they can be enjoyable.

While the body is identified with, emotions are suppressed and cause 'holdings' throughout the body. These 'holdings' are manifested in the experience of physical tension; people are so used to this feeling, they think it's a normal, natural way to feel.

When these 'holdings' dissipated in my body it was amazing to retrospectively realize how tense the body had always felt. No amount of stretching or relaxing had ever made my body feel like it was melting. Now the bodily experience can only be described as transparent, light and very vital.

When the Knowing 'happened,' that relativity is NOT Reality, the mind had difficulty understanding what has happened. That is, it was the mechanism that registered the Knowing, but there was no intellectual understanding of it.

It is very hard for people to understand that the mind is by nature peaceful. To most, the mind is considered the enemy and something to be battled with. But the battle is with involvement, not the mind.

When the false identity falls away, no experience is rejected or held onto. No experience is deemed important or desirable. No-one remains desiring anything and there is as much peace in washing dishes as there might be standing on top of mount Everest, watching the sun setting.

All experiences or feelings, however strong, arise and subside into peace. No thought is pursued or rejected. Thoughts still arise, but with no-one to latch onto them, they subside as easily. The mind goes about its job—planning and thinking—but is essentially peaceful, uninvolved.

The sense of time that preceded all this is no longer there. Each experience has a newness because it is uncolored by past memories. It is as if this whole story, and the story of the pseudo-identity preceding it happened but a moment ago.

Before the sense of presence is personalized, no-thing is considered personal. Then everything becomes 'personal' and the false self is superimposed upon what is natural. Self-realization signifies the absence of a knower and a known. There is no knower of the Self. There is no Self to be known.

The Knowing is beyond words, but the closest one can come with words is that all there is Is Consciousness or Experiencing. When this Knowing 'happened' the thought arose, "What is the Source of Experiencing?" For this question to be arising, it seemed the 'I' (individuality or innate personality) had remained, identified with Experiencing.

Unlike the 'me' object, which desired to Be the impersonal Subject, the 'I' did not desire its Source. There was simply questioning. Now all questions have ceased although it is clear that the *relative* process is incomplete.

When Self is 'realized,' the Knowing is still oriented to the body and mind. There is no longer the sense of the body as 'container' of awareness, but the body and mind are still the mechanisms orienting this Knowing.

When the mind no longer reflects the false personality, it can then be said that the intellect is a clearer 'mirror,' reflecting the Knowing of manifest-Self.

The understanding is there, that manifest-Self and the Absolute are not-two. However, until mind, body, and Knowing are transcended, there is still a relative on-going process.

To name the Absolute (non-manifest or para-Brahman) in which manifest-Self arises is to put words to that which cannot be talked about. Only when *all* concepts, including 'I' are 'transcended' can That which is beyond concepts, beyond duality, be 'Known.'

Your first concern as a 'seeker' is to realize 'I Am' minus labels. When all labels and identities have fallen away, this is the first 'step' only. What happens after this 'stage' is a deepening of dispassion—impartiality—as the mind turns further 'inward.'

It is rather strange to put all this into words, and clearly this is only a description of a relative process. However, preceding this story there were many misconceptions about how it might unfold. Perhaps in the writing of this it will help you put your present experience of self into a clearer perspective.

Minus censorship, the natural, innate personality was now expressing itself dynamically. Then gradually even the individuality—unique expression happening through the body—began to lose its definition.

At first I had no sense of the personality changes that were occurring. However, John and close friends expressed their perception of this personality change as very distinct. I found it strange that they expressed grief at this 'loss' of 'me'.

Then giving a Breakthrough workshop one-day, I realized how used I had been to communicating in a dynamic way. Suddenly it seemed most uncomfortable—and nigh impossible—to interact as before. The dynamism with which I was used to expressing myself seemed alien and quite exhausting.

When the essential nature begins to lose definition it is the habit of interaction that is falling away. You see, you are born with innate, natural personality traits. When interaction with the world begins, these characteristics become increasingly dynamic. This happens even before the personality begins to be modified according to the feedback of others.

When the dynamism behind interaction began to change, at first my mind interpreted it as a virus. That is, the body felt as if there was a core weakness. My body went from feeling extremely vital and light to feeling incredibly weak and my limbs felt heavy and numb.

This is when I realized that the mind had interpreted dynamic habits of self-expression as a source of strength. When this dynamism started to dissipate, the mind interpreted it as the body being sick.

Once this misinterpretation was understood, the body regained vitality and the process continued, and continues to this day. This relative change has also shown me, retrospectively, how much unnecessary energy was dissipated in interaction until this point.

This is not to say that others perceive me as a 'vegetable.' There is neutrality now, in which listening is total and receptive. From the standpoint of this neutrality, interaction still happens, but my perception of it is rather like ripples on a pond.

No Real difference was apparent between a 'me' and 'others' as before. However, until then, the uniqueness of expression through this body was experienced as distinct from that of other bodies. Now even this distinction is less defined.

When interaction is not happening, the 'ripples' subside and there is stillness. Thoughts still arise in the mind, but with decreased frequency. Emotions still arise, but infrequently and with less dynamism and little duration.

Remember, all these words describe a relative process only. This process is relative to this particular case and is not a prescription for 'awakening.' It is merely a description of the *relative* changes that the body and mind can undergo. They are of no significance because Reality is unaffected by them.

Even the description of relative processes is colored by the unique mode of expressing that is happening through this particular bodymind mechanism.

It must be understood that any communication that happens

is a filtering of the Truth. The Truth cannot be talked of.

It simply occurred to me to relate this story because, however different your process may be, some of you may find the relating of mine helpful.

Right now your mind may still be very much involved in its own *personal* story. If you consider yourself a seeker, know that becoming more aware and more knowledgeable is a misconceived goal. Awareness is all, and in it has arisen a false sense of self. Your essential nature is spontaneity—awareness. Your true nature is that which is now Knowing this awareness.

No-thing has been born, no-thing dies.

No-thing has free-will or any purpose.

No-thing has ever *really* happened.

If you do not Know this right now, it is only because you *believe* otherwise. The only 'goal' is to dissolve all goals. This will not happen as long as you are aiming to become any-thing. The idea of goals arose despite you, and can only subside despite you.

The Self is not a goal 'you' can attain. There is no seeker and no Sought. These concepts are only possible because of the perceiving principle which preceded them and in which they appear.

Between seeker and Sought is Seeing, Listening, Knowing, Being. If you deeply understand this, all that is left is to live life as it Is.

Note: In the following pages I have used the words sage (or Jnani) merely as a differentiation between one who is identified with the pseudo-personality and 'one' who is not. In this case, there is no longer a 'me' identity. To use labels to categorize and describe this absence makes no sense to me at all.

Within the limitation of language, labels have been used. These serve as differentiations between phenomenal appearances. These appearances have arisen within That which is undifferentiated.

I Am *neither here nor there,*
Neither this nor that.

Make Me *your goal*
And *find only yourself,*
Aiming.

Make Me *your prayer*
And *hear only yourself,*
Praying.

Be *as you* Are
And *there* I Am
Being.

Stop *thinking in terms*
Of *you and* Me.
Between *seeker and* Sought
Is Seeing.

E.V.

Satsang: Knowing yourself

The morning began with the question, "Why are you here?"

LS *I want to learn more about myself.*

EV Then I'm afraid you're going to be disappointed. You already know enough about yourself, and this is the problem. You already have a mind full of concepts and ideas about yourself.

If you come here expecting more concepts you have come to the wrong place. What will be said here will send all of them into disarray.

Are you happy with the way you feel and with your life right now?

LS *Some of the time.*

EV What happens the rest of the time?

LS *Things don't go the way I want, and I don't always deal with things the way I should.*

EV So, what you are saying is, you desire life, and how you are, to be different. Do you mean you would like to have more control over the way you act?

LS *Yes, I guess so. I feel out of control a lot of the time.*

EV What makes you think you can control anything?

LS *Well, I should be able to. I used to have quite a bad tem per, but it's not as bad as it used to be.*

EV Does that mean you are coping better with it now?

LS *Yes, I think so.*

EV It's interesting that the word cope means, 'to deal effectively.' Yet, when you talk of coping, don't you mean, you handle things better than you used to? As a result, do you feel happier more of the time?

LS *Well, I still stew over things, but I used to fly off the handle for nothing at all. That's better now. I'm not so quick to judge. I've learned to bite my tongue.*

EV The habit of over-reacting has decreased, but look how this happened. You 'bite your tongue.' This means you hold back your feelings. It doesn't mean you stop feeling agitated does it?

LS *No.*

EV So, what you call coping has nothing to do with 'dealing effectively' with situations does it? First you learned to judge, and then you learned not to judge outwardly. Did that dispel judging?

LS *No, I guess I'm still pretty judgmental, especially of myself.*

EV And in coming here, you hope to *learn* something that might make you feel better about yourself, is that it?

LS *Yes.*

EV Well, if you come here you must listen without filtering everything that is said through your mind and all its opinions. Don't effort to understand. You must listen with your heart and then what is ready to be absorbed will be.

All the judgments you have about yourself and life are 'coverings' of the heart. They don't allow you to have a direct and full experience of anything. When anything is interpreted via the mind, it can never be experienced fully.

Who you Really are, is unlimited and impartial. To have a direct experience of the That, the mind must first be empty of all dualistic concepts.

In the Bible the concept of enlightenment is talked of as,

'the peace beyond all understanding.' What this means, is precisely what it says, that no concepts remain. That includes the concept of enlightenment.

AJ *But how can the mind be empty of concepts. Aren't concepts thoughts and ideas?*

EV Yes, concepts are thoughts and ideas. Now, tell me about something that you know with absolute certainty. Tell me a thought you have about yourself, one that you know with absolute certainty to be true.

AJ *Well, I'm a woman.*

EV That is a label you have for yourself. Are you are absolutely certain that it is a truth—'I am a woman?'

AJ *Yes. I am.*

EV Where did that thought come from?

AJ *From my mind.*

EV Did you cause that thought to happen in your mind?

AJ *I suppose I learned it from my parents. My parents taught me about myself.*

EV So, do you think others can make you think a certain way?

AJ *Yes. When we are children our parents give us their beliefs. They teach us about stuff.*

EV But do your parents *cause* you to think? As a tiny child, did you *cause* the first thought that arose in your mind?

AJ *No, I guess it just happened.*

EV It isn't possible to 'make' thoughts happen, is it? They just happen and follow each other in succession. One thought leads to another, but no thought can be said to come because of something you—or someone else—does, can it?

AJ *If I want to think about something, or have to think about something, I do.*

EV But if you want to think about something, doesn't the

43

thought, "I want," precede the other thoughts?

AJ *Yes.*

EV Now close your eyes and try really hard to cause a thought.

AJ *The mind goes blank. Yes, it's true I can't cause them!*

EV That is a great form of reverse psychology you see. People spend a lot of time trying to still the mind, but if you try hard to make it think, temporarily it shuts up. So, you see, all thoughts happen despite you. As a result of thoughts actions happen. Do you see that?

AJ *Yes.*

EV Now if thoughts happen despite you, can the actions that follow those thoughts be 'caused' by you?

AJ *Well, they aren't caused by anyone else?*

EV But, didn't you imply that other people often make you angry?

AJ *Yes, but I guess that's my own fault.*

EV So, here you are, saying that other people can make you feel and act a certain way. At the same time, you believe that you can make yourself act. You believe that actions happen with personal volition, because of you.

AJ *Well, I know it's my fault if I react to another person. I should be less judgmental, more easy-going.*

EV If you think others *make* you feel and act a certain way, you are saying they have power over you. This would mean that you blame them for how you feel. If you think it's your fault that you act a certain way, you are saying you are to blame. Either way, you are saying that you and others have personal will, personal volition, aren't you?

AJ *Yes.*

EV Now let's look at these beliefs a little closer. You have agreed that thoughts happen despite you, is that right?

AJ *Yes. I agree that I can't cause my thoughts, although I'd never really thought about it (laughing).*

EV You call them 'your' thoughts. Yet, you don't know how they happen or where they come from. Interesting isn't it, that you still think they are personal and 'yours.' No thought arises because of you, and you don't know how thoughts happen, or where they come from. Isn't it rather strange that you own them and call them personal? Do you often feel guilty about thoughts, as you do actions?

AJ Yes, sometimes.

EV What a mess, eh? You not only personalize something, the origin of which is unknown to you, but then you take the blame for it too. Understand that the ideas you have about 'it's my fault,' have also happened despite you.

AJ I sort of understand, but it's a bit confusing.

EV You see, you came here wanting to learn more about yourself. Already you find yourself understanding less. That's good. With all the knowledge you had about yourself, you were still not experiencing peace. Within that knowledge there are judgments and, consequently, guilt.

This tells you that knowledge hasn't been helping you much doesn't it? So, what makes you think more knowledge is going to make you feel better?

AJ Hmm, I guess it can't, but how does one get rid of knowledge? When you know something it's there. Even if you change your beliefs, that's still knowledge, new information, isn't it?

EV Yes. And, just because you think differently about something, it doesn't erase previous beliefs. This is the danger of the power of positive thinking.

It's a wonderful method of raising self-esteem and feeling better about yourself. The trouble is, once self-esteem is better, people go on using the tool of affirmations.

Now, if a tool works well, it does the job and you stop using it.

You wouldn't use a hammer to bang in a nail, and then keep on banging the nail, would you?

AJ *No.*

EV If a tool is efficient, it does the job. Then the job is done and you put the tool aside. If you need to keep on using a technique, one has to assume it isn't getting the job done.

Similarly, if you *need* to keep on telling yourself something, mightn't it be a sign that you aren't getting the message?

AJ *Yes, I guess so.*

EV If you keep on needing to affirm something positive to prevent old ways of thinking, one has to assume, the old ways haven't been obliterated. Even if you aren't using a technique to change old thought patterns, every time you opt for a new belief system, it doesn't mean the old one has been erased. All that has happened is that the old way of thinking is being suppressed.

If you learn a rigid rule or doctrine when you are small, you often replace it with an even more rigid one. For example, as a child you learn that "a woman's place is in the home—barefoot and pregnant." If you see your mother as being unhappy, it is likely that you'll interpret this belief in a woman's place as a negative one. So when you grow up, you may well rebel against this idea and become a feminist.

The more rigid the beliefs you are programmed with as a child, the more rigid your beliefs will be as an adult.

On the one hand you might conform and throw yourself into the designated role—be it religious, social or otherwise. On the other hand you can rebel, and go in a totally different direction. Either way, you are reacting to programming and the actions you take are probably going to be extreme and possibly fanatical. You have new beliefs, but it's the old belief that is still dictating how you act.

AJ *I can see that. I'd never thought of it in that way. So what you are saying is that, the programming we receive as children never stops affecting us in some way. That's for sure.*

EV If you understand that, you'll understand that most people's lives are dictated by the beliefs they gained as little three, and four year olds. This includes people who are running countries, religions, huge companies, etc. Pretty scary isn't it?

AJ *Yes, it sure is.*

EV It may seem that one person influences another. If you understand that no-one is responsible for their thoughts, that changes everything doesn't it?

BG *Well, in that light, wouldn't it mean that we might as well all act irresponsibly?*

EV Listen again to what I'm saying. Thoughts happen *despite* the individual. These thoughts dictate actions which cannot happen 'because' of you, because the thoughts that lead to them happened despite you.

BG *I don't get it. If everything—thoughts and actions—happen despite us, that means no-one need take responsibility for their actions. That would lead to chaos, people killing each other and stealing. No-one would feel guilt and so, why wouldn't everyone just do what they want to?*

EV When you feel guilt does it help you to act in an efficient way?

BG *No, usually I can't think straight. All I can think about is what I feel guilty about.*

EV So guilt serves to make actions inefficient and often serves to stop you taking any action.

BG Yes. Or I act irrationally, trying to justify my actions.

EV Would you say, that when guilt is there you feel chaotic inside?

BG *Yes.*

EV   Aha, so here you are saying, "If I am not responsible for my actions there will be chaos." In almost the same breath you tell me that feeling responsible, or guilty for actions, brings about chaos. Do you see the dilemma you are in with this type of thinking?

BG   *Yes. So, what can I do about it? I can't change my thinking because that won't erase guilt. I don't cause my thoughts, so who am I to change them anyway? Seems like a huge catch twenty-two.*

EV   Good, this is exactly what you are in, a huge catch twenty-two. That is your mind is in a catch twenty-two, but You aren't. The only reason you think this dilemma is personal, is because you think your actions are a product of personally caused thoughts. Added to this you think that both the mind and actions define you, or are you.

At the same time you think that 'you' are this body, doing the actions. You look at the gender of the body and think, "I Am a woman." Then all the beliefs you have about this gender are added to your description of who you think you are. 'I Am sexy,' 'I'm a brunette,' 'I shouldn't be like this,' 'I should be like that.'

BG   *Yes, I have a lot of strong ideas about who I am and how I should and shouldn't be.*

EV   Now, you agree that the first thought that ever came into your mind happened despite you. From that thought sprung others, until your mind was full of labels and images of yourself. Now, you've personalized all those ideas and use them to describe yourself. All these descriptions of yourself are summed up in the little word 'me,' aren't they?

BG   *Yes.*

EV   How do you know this 'me' you describe yourself as?

BG   *I just do. I know, 'I am,' and call myself 'me.'*

EV   How do you know that you are?

BG *I don't understand. Because I'm alive.*
EV How do you know you are alive?

BG *Because 'I am.' I experience myself, being. I have a body and know it's mine and it's alive.*
EV What makes the body feel alive?

BG Well, the life force within it.
EV If you were to give this life force a name what would you call it?

BG *Universal life force.*
EV Do you think of yourself as universal, or do you think of yourself as being here, in one place, sitting on that chair.

BG *I know I'm here, sitting on a chair. Yes, I guess I don't think of myself as universal exactly. No, I think of myself as me, here and now.*
EV So you think of yourself as both the life force, and this body, is that it?

BG *Yes.*
EV How can you be two things at once?

BG *Well, I'm a combination of things. I have a mind, a body, life force.*
EV How can you Be something you say you have, or own? Who has this life force? Who has this body? Who has this mind?

LS *Phew, this is confusing.*
EV Good, we are unraveling a little more of these rigid ideas you came with. Now tell me BG, how do you experience being? How is it possible for you to experience yourself?

BG *Because 'I am.' 'I exist.'*
EV Could this body exist without the experience of being? If there were no consciousness in this body would it still be considered alive?

BG No.

EV Did you cause yourself to begin breathing, and having the sense 'I Am?'

BG No.

EV Was the body alive before awareness animated it?

BG *No. It was born with awareness.*

EV As a tiny baby there was just awareness. The mind contained no thoughts, no even the though 'I Am,' did it?

BG *No. I just was.*

EV So, first there was just awareness. Then came the awareness 'I Am.' Then the recognition of a body, different than others, happened. This body was recognized by others and called cute, or pretty. Then you were told, "You Are a girl," "You Are like this," "You should be like that," etc. These labels were then added to the sense, 'I Am,' and you began to think, "I Am some-thing," isn't that so?

BG *Yes.*

EV You needed others to tell you what you are, but did you need them to tell you that you exist?

BG *No, I figured that out on my own (laughing).*

EV So, the only thought that came to you, without you needing to have it affirmed was, 'I Am.' Even if you learned these words, you didn't need anyone to give you the experience of being, did you?

BG No.

EV That experience was there without any help from others. The 'help' you then received served to put the sense 'I Am' into a framework. As you grew up, you learned 'I Am a teenager,' 'I Am an adult,' etc. This means that the identity you began with has changed many times.

If a lump of gold is fashioned into a bracelet, then a ring, then a pair of earrings, how would you tell a blind person what it is?

BG *It's whatever it is at the time I guess.*

EV If a lump of gold changes appearance does it stop being a lump of gold?

BG *No.*

EV If you have liposuction or a sex change, or lose a limb does your body stop being your body?

BG *No.*

EV So, the basic body object is flesh and bones, and even when it is modified, it is still a body.

BG *Yes.*

EV When the body dies, does it stop being your body?

BG *Well, it's my body, but I'm no longer in it, so I don't call it mine or 'me' anymore. I'm not there to call it mine.*

EV What caused you to call it 'mine' in the first place?

BG *The fact that I experience it. The fact, that I'm in it.*

EV Who is in it?

BG *I am.*

EV How can you Be something you own? That doesn't make any sense does it?

BG *No.*

EV In order to own something you have to be separate to it don't you.

BG *Yes.*

EV When you say 'I Am,' who is this 'I' you talk of? How do you know about this 'I?'

BG *Because 'I' am. Because, I experience this body.*

EV Do you experience the body because you *are* the body?

BG *Well, no. I experience it because I'm alive. I understand that I can't Be something I own, so I can't Be the body.*

EV Good, so this is a new understanding. Now tell me, who is alive?

BG *I am.*
EV How do you know you are alive?

BG *Because I experience being. Because I have a body.*
EV Because the body is there you experience being. But the experience of being causes the body to feel alive doesn't it?

BG *Yes.*
EV If the experience of being causes the body to be alive, how can you Be the body?

BG *Well, I'm not, I'm just me, the sense 'I Am.'*
EV But what causes the experience 'I Am'?

AJ *I'm totally confused.*
EV You came here believing, 'I am a woman,' 'I am this person sitting in a chair,' etc. Now I am asking how you know this. You realize you know this because you experience being. This experience preceded all the labels you have for yourself didn't it?

AJ *Yes.*
EV Most people's identity lies in an ever-changing thing; the body. This is why everyone spends their lives re-inventing themselves. Today I'm a child, today I'm a business woman, today I'm successful, today I'm a failure.

Each time a change happens to the body and to your roles, you think, "I was this, and now I'm that." The body is an ever-changing object, the basic elements of which don't change.

If you are going to describe a lump of gold that has been fashioned into various shapes, you have to describe it according to its essential nature—gold—don't you?

AJ *Yes.*

EV So let's get you quite clear on the misperception you have had, until now, of being the body. If you are the body, which is always changing, to describe yourself truthfully, you'll have to say, "I'm a lump of flesh and blood, full of waste products."

AJ *Yuk.*
EV Is this what you think you are?

AJ *No.*
EV When it's put that way you don't like to identify with the body at all do you? If I chopped off your arms and legs and separated the head from the torso, would you be the head or the torso?

AJ *Well, I'm my heart.*
EV Ah, so you are an organ? What about the other organs and the waste products in the body? Are you sure you aren't any of those things? You see, when you scrutinize the idea you have had of yourself it doesn't make any sense.

AJ *No.*
EV The body functions, breathes, has five senses, pees, digests. Do you cause these functions to happen?

AJ *No.*
EV These functions happen despite you. You don't sit down after a heavy meal and think, now I'll make myself digest. You don't wake up in the morning and focus all day on making yourself breathe. The only time you focus on those functions is when they aren't working properly, when there is dis-ease, yes?

AJ *Yes.*
EV When any form of discomfort is present you focus on it, and effort with it. When you are feeling peaceful, you don't effort in any way do you? Until the mind thinks "how long can this last?," you just enjoy the experience don't you?

AJ *Yes.*

EV When you experience lack of peace, that's when you start asking, "Why?" Even if you are experiencing peace and then ask, "Why?," immediately the peace is gone.

Now, what percentage of your life do you spend giving meaning, looking for explanations and reasons, and justifying what you do and say by explaining it?

AJ *Phew, well, much of the time.*

EV You see, when you feel peaceful there is no need to look for meaning, or ask, "Why is this happening?" The only time you ask 'why?' is when you are not feeling peace. Both questions and the need to come up with answers, could then be described as a dis-ease state.

You are not at-ease with yourself or life, so you question everything.

When actions happen spontaneously, without censorship, there is peace. Spontaneity is lost the minute you start asking 'why' and 'how' and giving reasons. Then there is involvement and peace is absent.

AJ *Yes, I see. So, much of the time I'm involved.*

EV What you must remember is that even the censorship, and the involvement happen despite you. That is, even when you are efforting, and censoring thoughts and actions, that effort and censorship is impersonal. Involvement is the only 'problem.' The addiction to involvement with the 'me' is what blinds you to your true nature. What you must discover – un-cover – is who you are beneath all these labels. To do this you have to discover what the perceiving principle of these labels is. As you can perceive and conceive of these labels, you have to be separate to them. You cannot Be a label. You cannot Be a bunch of ever-changing concepts. This is simple logic. So, find out who you are not, and there you will have the answer to who you Really are.

Satsang: Mind Games

Q. *I have been noticing that since Breakthrough and coming to satsang, situations happen. They are situations that would normally have bugged me, but now they happen and I just think, "Well, that's what's happening."*

A. That's good, that behavior is less reactionary. But, don't let the mind trick you. It is a trickster that loves complacency. The pseudo-personality the mind calls 'me,' is self-satisfied. When it becomes dissatisfied it quickly looks for ways of regaining complacency.

You see the mind loves the drama of the 'me.' This keeps the mind addicted to drama and involvement.

So the thought comes, "Well, that's what's happening." Doesn't your mind take pleasure in this? Doesn't it enjoy this idea of detachment?

Q. *Yes, I guess so.*

A. The mind wouldn't even think, "Well, that's what's happening," or comment on it at all if there was no involvement. If what was happening was totally accepted, and fully experienced, the mind wouldn't be commenting on it.

Q. *Yes, I see what you mean.*

A. The fact that the mind has a comment which brings you pleasure signifies there is involvement. You may not appear to be involved in the situation, but the mind has found another involvement. It's involved in the pride it takes in having detachment.

There is nothing wrong in feeling pleasure and a little more detachment, but you must realize what is happening. The mind is still commenting on what it considers personal 'progress.' If real 'progress' had been made there would be no mental involvement at all, do you see?

Q. *Yes.*

A. The witnessing of the situation would be impersonal and so there would be no-one to take pride or even feel pleasure in detachment. As long as the mind is commenting on your 'progress' there is attachment.

Q. *Yes (sighing). So really no progress has been made at all.*

A. If there is a decrease in reactionary behavior, you might call this progress. But remember, the mind loves to regain complacency because it gives it a sense of control.

The pseudo-identity appears to be doing better, but as long as *it* is being attributed with the improvement, there is involvement.

To prevent the mind from feeling it has made an achievement, you must question, "How is the perception of this improvement possible?"

You were present before any thoughts entered the mind weren't you?

Q. *Yes.*

A. This means that your body functioned just fine without thoughts. Actions happened spontaneously. Then thoughts came in and you thought, "I Am." This thought was followed by descriptions of that Amness: 'I Am this, I Am that.'

As soon as the Amness was described, actions became less and less spontaneous. Instead you started describing the actions: 'that was good,' 'that could have been better.'

Actions became 'personal,' and personal efforts took the

place of impersonal, spontaneous actions. This is the beginning of the dis-ease state.

You are no longer at-ease with yourself because you think your body and its actions are personal. Then, comes effort and the need to control.

Q. *(another participant) I feel guilty when I see that I am taking pleasure in my progress.*
A. So question the guilt. How does this thought of guilt arise? Am I the cause of this thought?

Q. *No, it happens despite me.*
A. So, if the thought about guilt happens despite you, it is impersonal. Then where is there any-one to feel guilty about anything?

You see, your enquiry must not cease. Your enquiry must be untiring. This doesn't mean you need to analyze yourself. This process has nothing to do with analysis.

The mind is always concerned with your evolution, your future, how you will become. What must concern you, if you want to know the Self, is involution.

The mind must turn away from its interest in the 'me' and its dramas. To do this you have to keep on returning to the same place—thoughts happen despite you, therefore are impersonal. Question all thoughts, all involvements. Don't let the mind become complacent. As soon as you think you have made progress, question this thought. It is an involvement and belongs to the personalized identity. This personalized identity obscures your impersonal identity, the Self.

Q. *Yes, I see.*
A. When the body is thought of as 'me,' and thoughts and actions are thought of as personal, the need to control begins. Control, involvement, neediness, and victim consciousness are all synonymous.

The personalization of actions and the idea that you are a

'thing,' keep you stuck in the drama. Find out how this drama is possible. What is the perceiving principle of this drama? When you know that, the drama will end. It was never real, as no drama is real, but right now you think it is reality.

You have many desires in a lifetime. Some are realized, and some are not. None of them bring you everlasting fulfillment or peace. Because they are not eternal they are of no use to you.

Q. *Often I find my mind thinking about how life will look in the future.*
A. Such thoughts are limited to space-time, and concern you only because you are identified with a body, which is limited to space-time.

You are not a 'thing' and you never have been. In order to perceive any-thing you have to be separate to it. This logic alone tells you that you can't be a 'thing.' You can only be that which is prior to thingness, prior to all concepts.

As you are not a 'thing,' one could say you are nothing. As nothing, how can you ever have been born and how could you die?

Q. *I couldn't.*
A. Fulfillment of desires is fleeting. Life in a body is fleeting. When the body is 'dead' and the sense 'I Am' disappears, who cares about what 'you' have gained in life? Why all the interest in gaining fleeting experiences?

Your only concern, and one could say, your only worthwhile purpose in this body—as the mind loves to have a purpose—is to find out who you were before this body. Who were you before this 'Amness'?

Once you deeply acknowledge the temporary nature of the 'me,' you want something permanent. So, you think up ideas about reincarnation and soul migration and the like. This entertains the mind, but it doesn't give you any satisfying answer as to the meaning of life.

Q. *Well, does life have a meaning?*

A. If you are no-thing why would you need to have a purpose or meaning. It's only because you think of yourself as a 'thing' that you want meaning. It's only because you are identified with a 'thing' that you think in terms of a 'thing' that is born, dies, and is reborn.

Things—objects—by definition, are inanimate. So, how can a 'thing' go anywhere unless it is animated? You think you are the body-object and its animation. Logic tells you that isn't possible. No thing can animate itself.

When you understand that you can't be a self-animating object, you want to know how the animation is possible. God might be an answer for you, but God is a concept you have never seen. If you were God and could make people, would you give them the ability to act of their own volition?

Q. *Well, I might.*

A. I imagine you've all seen Frankenstein movies. There the creator creates a monster that has personal will and wreaks havoc, and turns on his creator. If you were God would you risk that?

Q. *I guess not.*

A. The mind finds a million reasons as to why you are here. Yet today you have perhaps discovered that you don't even know who you Really are. Once this understanding deepens, the mind will lose interest in evolution—becoming—and seek its source. The mind will begin the process of involution.

Then the desire to know Self becomes all you think, eat, drink and care about. The pain of this desire can be intense, but you cannot let it go because it's all-consuming. With this desire, all other desires are diminished. That is the good news. You care only about knowing Self.

59

Once you realize that Self is beyond concepts—non-conceptual—the mind squirms. As it can only conceptualize, it can never Know the non-conceptual Self.

Then the desire to be free of the (mind's) desire to know Self happens, because you recognize that ANY desire is involvement. Like all desires, this desire has come about despite you, and therefore it can't be dropped *because* of anything 'you' do.

Q. *So there's nothing we can do? There is no way of understanding who we are?*

A. No. The mind cannot conceptualize the non-conceptual Self. When you understand this, the mind goes in faster and faster circles. Eventually it knows beyond a shadow of a doubt that it can never understand who you are. In the moment it stops desiring to understand, in that moment, the Knowing of who you are is there.

All you can do is deeply understand that all understandings happened despite you. That no understanding is personal or holds any truth about who you are; understand that you cannot understand Self. That is the only understanding—to know beyond a shadow of a doubt that you know nothing that holds any truth about you.

Q. *But how can we go beyond understanding? That's all the mind knows how to do, understand and not understand.*

A. Ah, but the mind always thinks it can come up with an ultimate understanding for everything doesn't it?

Q. *Yes, it likes to think so. It's always trying, that's for sure.*

A. You can't stop control with control. You can't stop struggle with struggle. However, you can transcend the mind if you use the power of discrimination constructively.

Q. *Are you saying that you can use the mind to get rid of the mind?*

A. It's not the mind that is the problem. It's the mind's involvement that is the 'problem.' The mind is full of ideas about who you are. It thinks you are a body—a mind, a spirit, a woman, etc. Until now the mind has discriminated in a way that was unconstructive. It filled with ideas about who you are and made actions personal.

It discriminated between this action and that, between fat and thin, between right and wrong. This form of discrimination has been unconstructive to you, because it has given you feelings of guilt and pride—involvement.

Q. *Yes.*

A. Until now the thinking processes of the mind haven't been constructive. The only 'construction' the mind has made is the 'me,' the pseudo identity. This is a faulty perception, an illusion.

The mind has the power of discrimination. This power has got you in the mess of identifying with the body, and with the mind. It has got you into the mess of rejecting this and clinging to that.

The good news is that you can use this same power of discrimination constructively. With the mind, begin investigating everything it considers real. Already you have realized today that the idea of personal thoughts is a misperception, haven't you.

Q. *Yes. Until today I had never thought about any of this.*

A. You recognize that in order to perceive something you have to be separate to it. This means that you cannot Be any concept—not a body, not a mind, not a spirit. You can't Be thoughts or actions and roles either. You can't Be a business woman, or a homemaker.

Q. *O.K. I understand that.*

A. Discrimination means the ability to differentiate. Already today you have begun using the power of discrimination constructively. You have begun to differentiate between what is real and what is unreal.

In this way, the mind has actually begun deconstructing the 'me,' and the ideas you had about who you are. In this

way, the mind is deconstructing its habitual way of thinking.

Q. *So, you can use the mind to get rid of the mind?*
A. You can use the mind to get rid of involvement. That is, if
you investigate the beliefs you have about 'this is how it is.'
As the mind gradually realizes that it has been
misperceiving everything, the questions escalate.

Q. *So, involvement actually becomes more then. It gets worse?*
A. Yes, the mind is then totally involved, obsessed by this new
way of thinking. But unlike habitual involvements, which
take it from one extreme to another, the mind is aiming at
one ultimate extreme. It wants to know who the non-
conceptual You is. When it embarks on this it eventually
realizes the paradox of seeking the non-conceptual with
concepts.

This doesn't stop it trying to understand. The biggest
paradox is that the mind's involvement in seeking the non-
conceptual 'absorbs' all other involvements. The mind can
think of nothing else but understanding the Self.

Do you see that in this way the mind is deconstructing
itself? Through involvement it is now moving toward
dispassion, impartiality, and non-involvement. This is the
biggest paradox, yes. The mind is using involvement in a
way that will terminate involvement!

Q. *It sounds so complicated.*
A. Well, has your mind ever been non-complicated?

Q. *No. Well, rarely.*
A. When the mind is involved it Is complication. If you have a
complicated puzzle, the mind feels confused. Within that
confusion it searches for a solution doesn't it?

Q. *Yes. At least it tries.*
A. And when you solve the puzzle it is no longer a puzzle is it?

Q. *No.*

A. The mind can only solve the puzzle of who You are by investigating that which instigated all the confusion. The mind must investigate who you are not, the puzzle it has come up with.

It can't conceive of a non-concept, but it *can* investigate the concepts that define you. If you become clear on who you are not, what do you think will remain?

Q. *Who I am really.*
A. If you think a shadow on the wall is a monster, and then discover it is just a shadow, what has changed?

Q. *The way I see it.*
A. Has the shadow changed in any way?

Q. *No.*
A. No. The object of perception was always a shadow. What has changed is the way in which it is being perceived.

Similarly, when you find out who you are not; that you have never been a concept, what has changed? Have You changed in any way?

Q. *No. The way I see myself has changed.*
A. That's it. The mind's way of perceiving you right now, is faulty. When the mind realizes you aren't a concept what will happen to the mind?

Q. *It will stop conceptualizing?*
A. It will give up putting labels on you. It may continue conceptualizing a great deal at first. Then, gradually, it conceptualizes only when it is necessary to interact in the world. But, as there is no-one—no concept—to label, it won't be involved in any thoughts or actions. You won't feel guilty if You are no-thing, will you?

Q. *No.*
A. Minus 'personal' involvement, the mind will function efficiently when it's needed.

63

So yes, you can use the mind to go beyond involvement; to find out who you are not. You have so many labels for yourself that this will keep the mind busy, eh?

Q.   *Yes.*

A.   And it may suffice that you 'get' that everything happens despite you, spontaneously. This 'understanding' may be enough that you can simply go on with your life, doing what you are doing. But, as the mind is addicted to thinking, I'm proposing something constructive for it to do.

There are those engaged in strenuous exercises, abstinence, and other pursuits, trying to know the Self. Much of the time the pride they take in these practices, and the idea of 'becoming more spiritual,' serves only to strengthen the 'me' idea.

As the illusory 'me' idea is what is obscuring the Real you, these practices risk doing the very opposite of what is desired.

The process I recommend, of deconstructing thinking processes, isn't for everyone. This process is called *jnana yoga*. It doesn't allow the mind to puff itself up, and fall in the trap of feeling it is 'attaining.' It keeps the mind alert, and even humble, because it is a process of un-learning, un-attaining.

This is a process of involution, not evolution. It's a process of deconstructing through constructive thinking. There you have it, the ultimate paradox, eh?

Q.   *Phew, yes, it sure is.*

A.   IF you can keep it simple, just keep on doing what you are doing. That is all you can do, and all you have ever been able to do. Whatever 'you' decide happens despite you. Whatever you 'do' happens despite 'you.' When you understand this deeply all questions will cease. When this happens you will Know, 'beyond all understanding,' who you Really are.

The Mind

Like a hammer that bangs
To drown out the noise it makes,
The mind numbs me with logic
And philosophy.
When will it tire of all this?
Words, words, words.
The mind seeks to describe You,
And in so doing misses
The point it sought to make.
The voice of the heart
Is tried and convicted,
Guilty of longing and
Sentenced to silence.
The judge and jury
Continue to rant and rave.
Oh mind, when will you
Tire of all this?

E.V.

Conscience is the boxing ring
in which good and bad are pitted
against one another.
Guilt is the biased referee
we keep on the payroll to
mediate between our shoulds and
should nots and to ensure
that all fights are fixed
before they even begin.

E.V.

When you understand
you Know nothing

So often people tell me they want to feel 'One with everyone and everything.'

The term 'we are One' is given such frequent lip service that I feel the concept deserves some investigation.

Perhaps, when you say, "We are One," you are referring to the Essential nature. In most people this conflicting grouping of words denotes a misunderstanding. This is clear when I question people as to what they mean.

How can the word 'we' go hand in hand with 'One'? Clearly, 'we' denotes duality, while the word 'One' signifies its opposite. At best this phrase highlights the human being's battle with paradox.

While the idea of a 'me' and 'others' exists, most people can only think in terms of an idealistic state. My sense is that 'enlightenment' is thought of as an altered state in which all relative differences disappear. If this were the case why would I stay with my husband? If I saw no difference between John and my next door neighbor why would I choose to stay with one rather than the other?

It is idealistic to think that 'awakening' denotes the disappearance of relative differences. The objective world does not cease to appear to me. In fact, the richness of variety that I perceive is more vivid than ever.

If I saw no relative differences between myself and others, how would I be able to function? Who would pass the salt to whom?

Essentially there are no differences, and there is no separateness. When this is Known it doesn't dispel the appearance of my body sitting across from another body. It is very clear to me that my body is different to yours and that my body is female. If this were not the case, then most definitely you could say I am in an altered state. This altered state would make me non-functional as a relative individual.

The desire to feel 'Oneness' arises because you don't like feeling separate. When this desire is voiced as wanting to 'feel One with every-one' it almost always indicates an idealization of 'enlightenment.'

As long as 'others' appear Real, all the mind can do is cope with the perception. It gives itself affirmations such as, "We are One" hoping they will dispel the idea of separateness. What it wants most of all is to feel totally, permanently 'in control' of life. Of course, this is not the explanation you admit to yourself.

When coping happens it is always because you are unable to look beyond rigid ideas. An affirmation is a phrase that basically denotes 'this is how it is!' If you use affirmations it is because you are trying to eliminate one mode of thinking by implementing another. However positive you may think your new phrase is, it is nothing more than an addition to your arsenal of beliefs.

You see 'others' as separate to you and cannot see it any other way. You have heard it said that there is no difference between 'you' and 'others' and you desperately want to Know this. Until you do, making statements that contradict your present experience will change nothing.

Just because you affirm something repetitively does not mean it becomes a truth for you. If you affirm something it is because you 'believe' it to be true. If you Know, beyond a shadow of a doubt, that something is true you don't keep on affirming it. Imagine going to the doctor and undergoing a lengthy exam. Finally the doctor emerges from his office and says, 'I am sorry Mr. Jones, but I have to inform you that you are a monkey, not a human being!'

Now you might be amazed, you might decide it's time you changed to another doctor. You might even burst out laughing. What you are unlikely to do is feel angry because the doctor is contradicting your belief. This is because you have no doubt that you are a human being.

When you are deeply comfortable with any belief, it makes no difference who contradicts it. You don't need to go around justifying yourself or arguing with others who believe differently.

Conversely, when beliefs are underlain by doubt (albeit unconscious), you need to state them and justify them all the time. If you are using affirmations as a tool it simply denotes that you are uncomfortable with your existing thinking processes.

To think or affirm positively can be very beneficial—if you have spent your life thinking negatively. Once the mind has made some adjustments it gives you a whole new perspective on yourself. If you find that this perspective is reliant on constant affirmations it tells you that they have no permanent affect. It is time then, to rethink even the positive thoughts.

It usually becomes clear that what you 'understand' and what you experience are in conflict. Perhaps you 'understand' that you are 'not a bad person,' but still experience guilt. Perhaps you 'understand' that you are 'fine just the way I am,' but still feel the need to diet and have face lifts.

If your 'understanding' is that 'we are One,' it indicates a desire to see beyond relative appearances. As 'others' still feel very separate to 'you,' an intense frustration arises. The stronger this frustration is, the better—as long as you deal rather than cope with it.

To face the dilemma of 'separateness' head on, all understandings need to be put in question. If you understand 'we are One,' then think about what you understand. It means that there is an intellectual understanding that things are not as they seem.

So often people ask me questions and later I find they have developed a whole new language for themselves. Essentially what they have done is latched on to comforting phrases and taken them at face value. Then they use these words as if they are talking from experience and knowing. What has really happened is that they have discovered a whole new set of affirmations.

Here are some examples of the affirmations people use:

"Well, of course, I am not the one doing this!" They have 'understood' that there is no such thing as personal control or personal actions. *On the one hand they feel relieved because this gives them an escape clause from guilt. On the other hand guilt hasn't disappeared, so the new language serves as a way of coping.*

"I am not the doer, I'm being done by Source." This is a fairly loaded affirmation—as most are. They have 'understood' actions are impersonal, but still experience them as personal. *If they experienced impersonality of actions, actions would be spontaneous. There would be no need to justify anything that is happening.* By saying, "I am being done by Source," they are actually amplifying their belief in an 'I Am' that is separate to some-thing else.

To keep on affirming 'I am not the doer,' does not dispel the idea of personal actions. It might temporarily trip the mind up, but struggle will not have disappeared as long as this is being affirmed.

Another 'new language' people often adopt is the replacing of 'me' by the words 'this bodymind.' What they have 'understood' is that they Are not the body. If this were a Knowing there would be no need for strange language.

I don't now talk in terms of 'this bodymind,' but continue to say 'me.' I Know that I am not the body or the mind, so I have no need to announce this Knowing to the world by using strange language.

It is only when 'understanding' goes beyond the mind that it becomes a Knowing. The Knowing is that all concepts are relative, and no single concept is an ultimate truth. As long as you affirm ANY concept it is still quite clear you have only grasped an understanding. It is then easy to fall into the trap of replacing one understanding for another and concluding you have made progress.

Progress means 'moving forward' or 'moving beyond.' The trouble is what you are trying to move beyond is the idea that progress is necessary. You are trying to move beyond the belief that you need to be other than you Are.

Here you are, looking to dispel all differences between 'me' and 'others.' So what sense does it make to be struggling to Be different? All that is usually happening is that you are desperately trying to 'attain' some-thing for yourself. This self is the one that wants so much to be some-body special. Paradoxically, to Know who you really are is to realize You are no-body! This is very hard for the mind to come to terms with.

The Self has not identified with the 'me' for any particular reason. This is what is tripping your mind up, because it cannot let go of the need for a meaning. The mind loves concepts and wants more of them. 'I am not the doer,' 'we are One,' 'Source is doing me,' are all concepts—relative understandings. None of these phrases denotes that the 'me' knows anything. They simply signify that a new understanding has come about in relation to old beliefs.

The word *jnani* means 'one' who Knows. The Knowing has happened via a body and mind that the jnani is still identified with. There is a big difference between being *identified with* and *identified as*. The jnani Knows he or she is not the body. Because a body is still apparent, the Knowing happens in relation to that bodymind, although quite independently of it.

The term *ajnani* means one who does not Know. When the ajnani sits in front of the jnani and listens, two things can happen. If the mind desperately needs to understand something, a great deal of confusion results. This confusion can serve to throw all previously held beliefs into question. If the questions are pursued with discernment rather than rigid judgment, concepts will begin to fall away. The mind will gradually begin to understand it can never understand the Truth.

If the ajnani wants to understand so that he or she can 'attain' enlightenment, the ego (personal identity) is very much in the way. 'Attainment' is the ultimate, most prized goal, to the ego. The 'me' wants so much to feel special and 'enlightenment' is the ultimate ideal.

If the ajnani yearns to Know the Truth and that yearning is all-consuming, he or she will probably sit in front of the jnani experiencing tremendous pain. This pain is a bitter-sweet one because it signifies that the limiting experience of the personal identity is being felt to an extreme.

When you sit with someone who has a strong sense of personal identity you may also think you feel 'them.' This can be a wonderful or a grating experience, depending on how healthy the ego is of that person. The idea that others 'project onto you' is a perception only. All that is happening is that those aspects of your identity that need looking at are being felt more strongly.

Essentially, You are not separate to anyone. Until you Know this your experience of 'others' will keep on highlighting the belief in separateness. Either you will 'close down' and numb yourself to others, or you may be what is called 'a sensitive' and feel you experience everyone's emotions and pains. To 'sensitives' this is such a terrible experience that they find themselves increasingly avoiding others. Either way, the sense of separateness is being highlighted.

A personal identity no longer exists in the jnani. You may think when you sit in front of him or her that they 'radiate' or 'feel very powerful.' What you are feeling is not an individual, but the impersonal Self. This Self is not separate to you and therefore not isolated to the body of the jnani.

What is being experienced is the impersonal Self. This experience is happening within the Self that You Are. The jnani does not 'cause' this experience.

Relatively speaking there is great benefit to being with a jnani. When you meet with the common man, identities are traded. 'I am so and so,' 'I am this and that,' 'I am a business man,' 'I am a homemaker.' When you meet with the jnani he or she has no personal identity. The jnani may say 'I am a banker,' or 'I am an artist,' but Knows that this is not anything Real.

Many jnanis carry on regular lives and don't teach. You may unknowingly meet with one in day-to-day life, or you may meet with an overt teacher. Either way, when your personal identity is ready to fall away, the meeting will probably happen. If you meet with a jnani who overtly talks about 'his' Knowing it is probably because you are conscious of this falling away.

The thing to understand is that when the jnani appears it is because 'you' are ready to go beyond understanding. If you don't grasp this, the mind will sit there taking notes and adopting new beliefs.

The jnani is an embodiment of the impersonal Self. There is no essential difference between you and the jnani. The difference you experience is non-essential, relative. If you focus on the relative difference, it will cause the mind to yearn for equal 'specialness.' This will send it in circles trying to 'progress' and, in so doing, the mind will fill with more and more information.

"I am a person with personal control," is information. "I am not the doer," is also information. Information is a collection of concepts that denote an ideal. No ideal has any ultimate truth in it.

The Self is obscured because your mind is full of concepts about who you are. The jnani shows you the faulty perception these beliefs have given rise to. There is no point in adopting the jnani's words. The jnani is not telling you any Truth. He or she is merely pointing you away from everything you have believed in up until now.

The Truth of who you Are is beyond all concepts. This means that it cannot be put into words. All the jnani can do is tell you what you are not. If you go away thinking you have gained an understanding, do not rest on your laurels. Investigate the understanding until your mind realizes it has not grasped any truth.

The jnani embodies the Self that is You. In the embodiment of the jnani, the Self is not obscured by false identities. The identities you own, and sit in front of the jnani with, are not Real.

Do not go to the jnani searching for enlightenment or any other identity. Go understanding that you are ignorant of your essential nature. This ignorance has arisen in all the information you have accumulated about yourself. The ignorance of Self is only apparent because you are holding onto understandings about your identity.

You do not Know who you are, whereas the jnani does. The jnani Knows there is no essential difference between you and himself. He cannot tell you who You are, but he can help you see who you are not.

While there is understanding, you Know nothing. If you go to Satsang, with this 'in mind,' the mind is less likely to get in the way. Although the mind always puts up a valiant battle, it gradually recognizes that it is fighting a losing one.

Who You are is not a concept and so cannot be found by means of any concept. Concepts can point you toward Self because they describe who you are not. If you don't latch onto them, but investigate each concept that arises, you will discover they are all invalid. You experience yourself as a bunch of concepts and identities right now. The pain of this has drawn you to these teachings. Do not take them as gospel truth, or any truth at all. They are merely concepts that you must investigate ceaselessly if you are to Know the Truth that lies beyond them.

Circles of the Mind

Back in the sixties, in Switzerland, if one went to an interview the train fare and hotel accommodation were paid for. At the age of fifteen I did not relish interviews, but the lure of free travel and a chance to acquaint myself better with my mother's homeland was enough to tempt me to make a number of job applications throughout the country.

I mapped out an interview itinerary and managed to see most of Switzerland in the following four weeks. It didn't really occur to me that I might land a job and, funnily enough, I did not really have any vested interest in doing so. My focus was more on the adventure and having my first taste of autonomy.

Upon returning to England I fell in love with a young mathematics professor and, with this newfound distraction, my dreams of traveling took a seat on the back burner. It came as a shock to me then one Thursday to receive a letter in the mail, along with a one-way plane ticket, asking me to begin work on Monday in Switzerland.

Despite excellent qualifications, I was considered "too young to hold a position of responsibility." Consequently I found myself placed in a typing pool with little work, but an excellent salary.

At fifteen years of age I was living in luxury, with an idyllic apartment on Lake Geneva and the benefit of company skiing weekends. None of this was sufficient to stem my frustration with work. I sat down and calculated how much I would need before I could move on. Then I resigned myself to a diet of French bread and cheese for the next year and began to save. Others could try to limit me, but no-one was going to stop me living my dreams.

One day, whilst visiting a friend, he put on some music I had

75

never heard before—Greek music. My heart soared and I jumped up and announced, as much to my surprise as his, "I'm going to Greece." "So, I suppose if I'd put on Persian music you'd be going to Iran," he laughed. Who knows why I chose Greece, a place I knew nothing about, but that was how I came to make my next move.

A year to the day that I began work in Switzerland, I gave my notice. Boarding first a train, and then a ship, I sailed down the Gulf of Corinth and landed in Athens. The travel bug had taken hold and would continue to urge me further and further afield over the next twenty years. Whether I put a pin in the map, or met someone who told me tales of other places, I would simply up and move when the 'call to the wild' took me.

From my home in England the world had appeared so vast, yet once 'on the road' it seemed to be minus boundaries and just an extension of my little village. As soon as I began to feel settled anywhere I would always move on. I abhorred attachments of any kind—be it people or things. All my worldly goods fitted into one small hold-all and the sense of freedom was exhilarating.

Freedom was the key word for me and it seemed possible only as long as I remained non-attached. As the years, countries, and people passed me by, I began to realize that my life was punctuated by farewells. I loved the life I was living, but the cost began to accrue. In order to remain free I felt I had to keep on moving, but my memories had begun to mean more to me than the present moment. When I was in one country I would reminisce on the last one and plan for the next.

It was some sixteen years into my travels that I began to realize that the freedom I so coveted had become a limitation in itself. I remember lying listlessly on my bed watching the rickety old ceiling fan clanking around and around overhead. It looked and sounded as if it had spent its lifetime trying to work its way out of the ceiling. At this stage in its life the hot humid air of my room was no match for it.

I could not remember how many hotel rooms I had frequented, much like this one. How many cracked ceilings, how many naked light bulbs or rickety fans I had lain staring at. Another city, another hotel, and another country...they had all begun to blur. Today Paris, last year Hong Kong, tomorrow... It did not really seem to matter where I was anymore.

I was not sure when I had stopped feeling the enthusiasm for life I used to have. I used to live for travel, new countries, new people, and new experiences. I was the ultimate free spirit—free to get up and leave when I wanted, just like a gypsy. I did not have to answer to anyone. People envied my life, found my stories fascinating, and told me they only dreamt of the life I was living.

I could never understand them. Why didn't they just up and leave too. "It isn't that simple," they would say. "I have my job," "I have my boyfriend," "I don't have the money." To me all those were just excuses, one just had to have a strong enough dream and one could do anything one wanted. Nothing was impossible.

In the preceding months, the dreams seemed to have lost their meaning for me. I had realized most of them I ever had—all of them in fact. There had never ever been anything that did not eventually happen if I had once dreamt it strongly enough. I never considered this a sense of ambition or purpose. It was simply a matter of realizing dreams.

There on that day, in another hotel room, on another mattress with broken springs, I realized that dreams had lost their magic. Actually, I seemed to have lost all sense of dreaming. There was nothing at all I dreamt of—nothing.

The streets outside looked so colorful in the afternoon sun, with the hustle and bustle of the Nepali marketplace down below, replaying itself as it had done, probably for hundreds of years.

Out beyond the rooftops rose the Himalayas, as if standing sentry, guarding that little hubbub of humanity. I remembered sitting in geography class all those years ago, soaking up the names of places like Persia, Afghanistan, Nepal, and Siam. Rolling them around in my mouth, whispering them to myself. "Pipe dreams" my friends had said, but I knew better. The perfect career, the perfect marriage—none of that was on my itinerary, I just wanted to travel.

There I was, the Himalayan Mountains in my back garden, in Nepal, a place I had dreamed of with such fervor as a child! Why couldn't I feel anything anymore? Where was the wonder, the enthusiasm? I didn't feel lonely—it wasn't that.

Of course it was good to have someone to share a sunset with, or a traveling mate to share the adventures with. Most of the time, however, I had traveled alone, and liked it that way. One was more open to meeting the local people, without the distractions of having to worry about someone else.

No, it wasn't the loneliness or the being alone that was the problem. It was the emptiness, the limbo. Yes, the limbo more than anything. Plans for the future always helped. Dreams of the next place, and what it might hold, always made the empty times in the now seem more livable I mused.

That had always been my mode of handling life—having a Plan B at my fingertips when Plan A was becoming too familiar, to personal. Ah, too personal—that was the real story of my life.

When had the falling away of dreams started happening? Subtly perhaps, if I was honest with myself, for quite some years.

Some people fear change, hate change, and avoid change, of any kind. Many people I knew were happy to visit the same little beach in Majorca every year, where they know they can get eggs and bacon and meet other English people. Most people seem to like change if they can have the familiar to fall back onto. The vacation ends and they can go home, show off their tan, and show off their holiday snaps.

It all sounded so mundane to me. I had become a snob of a traveler—that was for sure. I had little time for tourists who dared put only one foot in the waters to test them and then jumped right back onto safe, familiar, dry land. I had always put a pin in the map, saved up, and gone wherever the pin landed.

I never read up on places before going to them either. I didn't want to have any expectations at all. I didn't want to have any ideas in my head as to what I might find as I stepped out of the train, or the ship, or at a new airport. Adventure was what I wanted, not the familiar, not the safe and definitely not to *need* anybody or anything.

There I was, my dreams spent, my memory banks spilling over with exotic countries and exciting travel stories. There I was, thirty-something years old, and what had really changed in me? Was I that much different to the tourists I so mocked? After all, after all these years of traveling, the unfamiliar was as safe and familiar to me as their way of life was to them. In fact, to lead a nine-to-five job and live in one place for more than a year represented a major challenge.

So perhaps I had come full circle—perhaps it was time to return to the point from which I had first set off—the familiar, the stable, the seemingly mundane. If it challenged me that much, I mused, then it, too, now represented the unknown. Why did the very idea of it terrify me so much?

As years went by the circles of my mind became increasingly hard to ignore. Eventually I 'bit the bullet' and entered into my first marriage. I was heavily armed with an arsenal of deep beliefs about freedom, wherein marriage appeared to be its antithesis. Needless to say, my marriage failed and lasted just over a year.

My brief, sad experience of marriage gave me enough insights into myself to show me the benefit of living with ones' polarity. I knew how easy it was to avoid the aspects I disliked about myself when there was no-one to provide a reflection.

In 1991, some 10 years after my first foray into marriage, I tried again. This time my partner, John, did not allow me the luxury of cowardice. Despite my occasional relapses into the 'caged bird' syndrome, through him I gradually realized that freedom had nothing to do with lifestyle and everything to do with attitude—or, perhaps, lack thereof.

As marriage was probably the precursor to a more concentrated investigation of self, it feels apt to begin mapping my 'journey' with the topic of relationships. Relationships provide a place I feel, for all of us, where we can most easily discover who we are and what we are about. This is primarily because relationships are the one arena wherein we have the greatest potential of discovering who we are NOT.

Relationships

If your relationship with your partner is one where you both inspire and support each other in change, you need read no further. For those of you who are still befuddled by the dynamics of relationships in general, or your present relationship, this may give you some insights.

As you probably already understand, flexibility of attitude is very helpful when it comes to relationships. If two people stick to their guns all the time, discord is all they will end up with. Whether you deal with discord by coping or overt arguing, you know that neither way is satisfying.

I'm not going to give you any method of ceasing discord. When two unique individuals get together, discord is always inevitable to some degree. This is because the differences between each of you are highlighted. Paradoxically, the gift of relationships is that they show you the aspects of your personality you dislike.

Most people think 'getting to know each other' is important. They think, "This will make us closer," but, invariably, as the old adage goes, familiarity breeds contempt. If contempt doesn't happen, boredom usually does. If one or both of you are master copers it's easy to stay numb to either feeling.

It really doesn't matter how many bunches of flowers or candle-lit dinners there are, if you have to work at maintaining the glow, you can be sure something isn't right.

People often talk of 'working at a relationship,' and for many, work is exactly what it feels like. This is because the idea of getting to know the other is usually what is being struggled with.

Have you noticed how, just when you feel you really know your partner, they do something that throws you totally off kilter? They have an affair, act violently, or just seem to ignore you or not understand you at all. Where good communication and love once reigned, suddenly all you find is confusion.

What's going on is that your knowledge of them is being contradicted. In your head you had a set of lists that described your partner. These made you feel secure and comfortable and, if you are honest, in control.

You may think getting to know your partner is important and valuable. What you may not have realized is that the need to 'really know' someone, is all about control.

I remember as a teenager and in my twenties, returning to England between travels and being told, "You haven't changed a bit." I desperately wanted them to see me in a different light. I wanted them to recognize all the changes I felt, but they didn't want me to be different. Within days, everyone was as irritated by me, as I was with them. Their rigid image of me was being challenged and I felt limited by this image.

Teenagers, in particular, will relate to this. They are usually experiencing constant and dynamic change. This is because they are still honing and wanting to explore all possible identities. If parents and friends keep on holding up 'their' idea of the child, there is nothing to do but conform or rebel.

To talk in honest language, getting to know someone, means having an ever-rigidifying picture of them. You want to deeply know them because familiarity gives you a sense of security—and control.

You 'know' exactly how they want you to act when you know their likes and dislikes. This is your decision to limit self-expression. When you get really good at it you then blame your partner for your own feelings of restriction. When you both master the art of interacting 'appropriately,' you mistake the comfort you feel for freedom. Then you wonder why love disappears.

Love begins when two people come together and each feels they can be themselves with the other. This feeling comes about because, initially, you are totally unfamiliar with the other person's identity.

There you are, two strangers, temporarily experiencing free-

82

dom from personal identities. At last you have found someone with whom you don't have to put on a front. As the love grows, the idea comes that you don't want this to end. As soon as you think of endings, the love becomes conditional.

We've all heard ourselves saying, "When I am with you, you make me feel..." As soon as these words are uttered we have made the other person responsible for our emotions.

You may enjoy being told, "You make me feel...", but in time this responsibility can become stifling. Each wants the other to continue 'making them feel' the same way. What a heavy trip to lay on anyone, but this is often what love ends up being—a heavy trip.

You decide the other person is responsible for your feelings and you like those feelings. To maintain the feelings, you think you have to hold onto the other person. So, you start telling them about yourself and they tell you about themselves. To succeed in keeping them, you think you need to add positive descriptions to their view of you. Gradually you each form a picture of the other. The getting to know each other process begins.

Where it was once possible for you both to be yourselves, suddenly you are being who you think you should be. You each give the other a picture of how you want them to see you, and then you have to maintain it. You give each other the good picture, and leave out the 'bad' bits.

At first, because you are being swept away by great feelings, it's easy only to show your good side. If you both do a good enough job of presenting a positive image, the love, albeit now conditional, seems to grow. Then perhaps you marry or move in together.

This is when it gets harder to keep up the facades. Where once you could be yourself, you find yourself having to be a certain way. When you and/or they aren't 'perfect,' the love seems to wane. In the early stages you may enjoy making up. Later on you find yourself either coping by masking your feelings or battling to communicate them.

Because we are all always experiencing change, we never feel the same from one moment to the next. Some people thrive on change, but most see it as a threat. This is why a stable love relationship is so appealing. Here you have someone who is in this stormy sea of life with you. Someone with whom you feel secure—as long as they aren't changing in ways that contradict your view of them.

When two people are rowing a boat together, they need to do so in synchronicity. They have to match their strength and row with equal, measured strokes. If they don't, the boat will probably just turn in circles. If one becomes tired, the other has to slow down a little. If one is stronger, he or she has to either row more gently or the other one has to increase their efforts. The only way balance is maintained is when the two people come to a compromise.

> *Marriage and long-term relationships are much like a rowing boat on the sea of life. They can provide you with a place that is stable because of its familiarity. If rigid ideas about each other accumulate, a relationship eventually becomes a potential* Titanic.

At first you adapt and compromise between your and their needs. Unfortunately, the image we have of our partner rarely keeps pace with the changes that happen in them. This means that their needs and yours are always changing.

This is when you find yourself exclaiming, "But you always...," "But, you never... ."

I think it was Lord Byron who wrote of his tailor being his best friend. This was because every time he visited, the tailor would re-measure him. In relationships, the greatest discord occurs when you fail to re-measure each other.

You like to think 'this is who you are.' Then you feel in control of the seeming 'cause' of your feelings. When the other person acts in uncharacteristic ways, immediately you fear the change. The person you know 'makes you feel' a certain way. If they change perhaps these feelings will disappear.

Other people offer you a mirror image of your own psyche. When they do something and you feel a certain way, they have not caused those feelings. The feelings are as a result of your attitude toward the other person.

When your feelings about another person change it isn't because 'they' changed. It is always, only, because your attitudes about these changes have triggered new feelings in you.

If you think it's important to know your partner well it is because you need security and control. You want the fairy tale to last and this means you both have to remain the hero and heroin of the tale. Yet few fairy tales are all bliss and joy.

There is always a protagonist somewhere in the story and usually a battle is fought before the happy ending. It's only because you think in terms of beginnings and endings that the idea of control ever arises. You feel joyful and suddenly find yourself thinking, 'I wonder how long this will last.' What you don't see is that at the beginning of every relationship, the conclusion is already there, in-potential. When anything ends, a new beginning is already there, in-potential. If you move toward something, you are, at the same time, moving away from something else.

While the desire to have an absolute and rigid definition of anything exists, you experience conflict. This is because you are avoiding the potential you expect, and to do this you must struggle.

One of the best places to see the desire for control in action, is in a relationship. When you think you 'know' absolutely everything about your partner they pull the carpet out from under you and change. If this causes discord you may battle to 'change them back.' "I just want the you I first met, not this person you are now!"

What you are saying is, I can't stand change because it makes me feel totally out of control. If you have to re-measure them it means you have to re-measure yourself. This is because you have put your two images together and called it 'marriage.'

This kind of marriage highlights all your feelings of limitation to the extreme. You began the relationship by thinking he or she 'makes me feel.' When your partner acts in uncharacteristic ways, your attitudes towards him or her change. When your attitudes change, so do your feelings. Immediately 'they' are to blame because you don't have that great, blissful love feeling anymore.

There is only the Self, unlimited, unbound, and free. When

you first met your partner the Self was not masked by identities. What happened was that all sense of limitation dropped away, albeit temporarily. There was a deep sense of peace, and the mind translated this and it became an emotion you called love.

You think you want to hang on to your partner because they are responsible for how you feel. You want the feeling of love, one-ness, and limitlessness, to last. The only way you think this is possible is if you keep throwing the image you like of them in their face: "This is how you are and I like it, so don't rock the boat!" If only people were that honest with themselves—and each other.

Although you may not realize it, the one-ness you desire has nothing to do with the 'other.' It has everything to do with wanting to know Self. Intuitively you know that Self is limitless and peaceful. Intuitively you know that feelings of separateness are an illusion.

The misperception you have of 'me' and the 'other' causes you pain. Your partner is always reminding you of this pain. Hence the need to only focus on the similarities between you.

When love wanes it is not too difficult to recognize that the pain you feel is one your partner shares. Love seems to have disappeared, and it seems as if the differences between you are insurmountable. As long as you focus on them, the feeling of separateness is exacerbated.

Heady, ecstatic feelings may be all you want, but all you feel is anger. Then it becomes impossible to meet each other half way. All you can do is blame them, and/or yourself and you are at deadlock.

Pain is what you now have in common. Keep on focusing only on the differences and no solution can be found. Recognize that you both feel pain and your focus will shift to a common ground. This is when communication, rather than defensiveness, can happen.

Instead of anger and confusion, compassion arises for both yourself and your partner. 'What a mess, what happened, let's see what we can do about it.' This is when you begin re-measuring each other and the relationship.

When re-measuring happens, a compromise is possible. Perhaps the only compromise you come up with is that you separate. You recognize that you both have rigid ideas that cannot be let go of. The compromise is that you give up the fairy tale in order to preserve your beliefs.

If you are clear with yourself on what has happened, this may teach you a valuable lesson about future relationships.

You began with openness and feelings of oneness. This is when you could only see similarities and differences you liked. You latched on to these and engraved them in stone in your mind. "This is who he is"! The picture you held in your mind then began conflicting with the one he or she presented you with.

Conflict never lies between two people. It always lies between your rigid beliefs about the other person and the contradictions they show you. Conflict is always an inside job, but until you recognize this, it is easier to blame the other person.

If you don't continuously re-measure others, you will always feel out of control and separate. While you are trying to control anything, you experience limitation. Just try pulling hard on the door knob of a locked door. If the door flies open you lose control and fall backwards. While the door stays shut you have no control over the door.

Control is an illusion and it is the one that relationships are continuously showing you. You can hold your identities up to each other and say, "Deal with it." This means that one of you will have to let go of control and compromise. Or you can both stand rigid and, in so doing, have no control over the other. When you both find a middle ground and compromise, it is because both of you have let go of the need to control. Then you maintain balance and harmony.

In nature balance and harmony happens through change. Can you imagine if a tree kept all its leaves and kept on growing new ones? Similarly, human beings are subject to change. They get old, wrinkles develop, they take up new habits, discard old ones. Human beings are not rigid, so to hold onto a rigid view of anyone is an impossible fantasy.

Each time a re-evaluation of your partner is required,
you have the opportunity of seeing how strong your need for
control still is. The need for control is what limits you,
not the other person. When you recognize this, you will
recognize the gift of relationships.

Each step of the way in a marriage requires bartering. You decide you want to take a job that requires you to travel. This means you'll be apart, but it also means that when you are together you'll be able to afford the vacation you dream of.

You decide you want to have children, but this means giving up the relationship as it is now. You will have less time for each other and, maybe, need to work harder. You have to weigh up what you will lose against what you will gain. Again and again you have to give up one way of being for another. This means you have to give up existing attitudes and relinquish the known for the unknown.

To desire knowing someone fully so that you can feel secure, is to resist the unknown. To resist the unknown, is to resist knowing Self.

You accumulate all your personal identities because you want to define yourself—'I Am this or that.' When those identities are rigid and you feel, "This is who I am," you feel secure. The feeling of control is so good you hang tight to those identities. If you have to hang tightly to anything, as you know, you must relinquish freedom.

You think what you do and how you look, is who you are. You think being a certain way will give you freedom. Yet as soon as you 'are' that way, you fear change. This is because you know change is inevitable. Within control, lack of control is in potential. Within freedom, limitation is in potential. If something is not an absolute, it is an illusion. An absolute describes 'not two'—which is the meaning of the Sanskrit word advaita.

The desire to bridge the separation between yourself and others is merely a reflection of the urge to know Self. Intuitively you know you cannot Be an ever-changing thing. Blindly you strive to discover something absolute about yourself.

While you have no true understanding of your resistance to

change you battle with it. You think it undermines you, as do changes you see in your partner. You desperately want all undesirable differences to disappear. This is the similarity between all people.

Recognize that everyone is in the same pain. No-one experiencing this struggle knows continuous underlying peace. Everyone wants the same thing—to feel peaceful, unlimited, and free. How can placing ever-more rigid identities on another or on yourself give you freedom?

The rigid identities you relate to as 'me' is what makes you feel limited. The rigid identities you give to others are what makes them feel limited. Clearly, you'll never know yourself or anyone else if you think ever-changing set of identities are who you 'are.' All you will ever know is an inconstant, inconsistent 'you' and inconsistent 'others.'

Deep love relationships always, at some point, result in pain. This usually happens very soon after love is felt. The ideas, "Can this last?," "I hope this will never change," always arise.

The similarity between you and your partner is that you want to be free of the pain of separateness. Right there in your seeming separateness there is a common ground.

The experience of Being is the only constant between seemingly separate individuals. If you focus on differences and uncontrollable changes you will only ever experience 'me' and 'others.'

Until now you have perhaps only focused on what you want to see and know about yourself. If this is the case, your view of others is probably beset by similar rigidities.

You don't know who you Really are, so how do you think
you can ever know who anyone else Really is?

Just think of a belief you held as a child. Perhaps your parents instilled this belief in you. As you grew older the belief may have changed. Then as an adult perhaps it changed again. Maybe you even realigned with your first belief.

Each time you hold a belief you think, "This is how it is." Now just look back at your life and realize how many conflicting personal truths you have held. This tells you that you can never be sure that any belief is an ultimate truth. This tells you that you know nothing for sure. No understanding is an absolute.

Stop trying to know your partner and battling the changes you see in him/her. The conflict in your mind is there to show you that nothing is certain. The love relationship is constantly showing you the fallibility of the mind.

The similarity between you and others is the pain of separateness. The desire to bridge it brings you together. Beingness meets Beingness and talks of being some-one. This some-one keeps on changing, but Beingness does not. Until you Know who you Are before all these identities appeared, you are identified with change.

If you fight change in yourself and your partner, you experience feeling limited. If you embrace all changes you will experience limitlessness. When neither of you need act a certain way, the unknown can be explored; then spontaneity of actions happens.

The rigid picture you hold of yourself will never disclose your True identity. What makes you think the picture you like of yourself or your partner is the best one? The unknown is only feared because it is beyond your control.

How crazy to desire freedom and think it is only possible
by having control. When controlling falls away, you
are still Being. The difference is you are not being a certain way.
This is freedom—being as you Are. When it happens,
you don't question why or how, you just enjoy it. When you
first fell in love and weren't yet questioning why,
or will it last, you experienced freedom.

Stop trying to understand yourself and others. Stop looking for knowledge of yourself in changing identities. If you do this, you will cease trying to know others via their identities. Then a relationship can fulfill its purpose. Then you are both able to Be as you Are, unrestricted, unlimited.

This is how the love experience begins, isn't it? For a short while you feel you and the other person are 'one.' Differences are immaterial because the similarity is felt so strongly. This similarity is that neither of you have is holding an identity up. Expression is free and spontaneous and you can be yourself.

Two seemingly separate selves come together and intuit their oneness. The only reason this Knowing disappears is because identities get in the way. The feeling of separateness has not happened because you are suddenly essentially different. *The separateness is felt because relative differences in identity are being focused on.*

The 'problem' lies in your focus on the identity you 'know.' Before you had any rigid knowledge of your partner, you embraced the unknown and felt one-ness. Recognize that knowledge of the other has blinded you to their limitlessness. Knowledge and understanding always gets in the way of the unknown.

Right now you do not Know who you are. Understand that the Self in you is the exact same Self as that in your partner. For a brief time you glimpsed this and this is why you are together. The Self knows no separation, no 'other,' no limitation. Both of you, albeit unconsciously, have come together to Know this.

"Mind creates the abyss.
The heart crosses it."
SRI NISARGADATTA MAHARAJ

Satsang:
Predetermination and goals

Q. *What do you think of the idea of predetermination? Do you think that everything is predetermined?*

A.   Will you feel better if I tell you that it is?

Q. *Well, I just want to know what you think about it.*

A.   As I am not an appearance; a body or a mind, I am not in the least concerned with the concept of time or predestination. If I am not limited in any way why would I have any concern as to what might happen within the realm of appearances? The only reason you are interested in predestination is because you believe you are a body, subject to a limited lifespan.

Q.   *But we have to have a purpose for being here. Is that purpose predetermined?*

A.   If I tell you that everything in life happens spontaneously, despite you, how does that make you feel?

Q. *Well, I don't think of it like that. People have to have a purpose and goals.*

A.   It's because you believe you have to have a purpose, and because you believe that goals are necessary, that you experience limitation. As long as you are goal-oriented you experience the need to control, and you experience distress when your goals aren't realized.

Q. *Well, I don't need to do anything, but I like to help others and feel I can help others. While I am in this body I want to help others.*

A.   Who is in your body?

Q.   *I am.*
A.   Who are you?

Q.   *I'm me. Me, myself and I.*
A.   Who is this 'me' you talk about? Is it the body?

Q.   *It's spirit, and the body and the five senses.*
A.   How can you possibly be all those things? What is this thing you call spirit?

Q.   *It's an ethereal being.*
A.   It's a concept. How can you be a concept? In order to conceive of, or perceive anything, you have to be separate to it don't you? Your eyes can't see themselves can they? How can anything see itself or affect itself? A TV can't see the pictures on its screen. You have to be separate to something if you want to see it. The concept of spirit is just a concept. How does the knowing of this concept happen?

Q.   *I know about it because it has come to me. My mind knows about it.*
A.   How did this thought come into the mind? How does any thought come into the mind? When you were a tiny baby, with a mind empty of concepts, how did the first concept, 'I Am,' arise in the mind? Did you make it happen?

Q.   *Well, I don't know, it just happened.*
A.   Exactly. The first concept arose despite you, despite any effort on your part didn't it.

Q.   *Well, yes, that I have to agree on.*
A.   After that first thought, did you start making thoughts come into your mind?

Q. *No. No, I didn't.*

A. So thoughts arise despite you, and you have no idea how that happens do you?

Q. *Well no, I guess not.*

A. Now imagine that you receive a blank envelope in your mail-box. It has no forwarding address on it, so you don't know where it came from. It doesn't have your address on it either, so you can't be sure it is really for you. Despite this, you take delivery of it and open it. Inside there are instructions as to how to act. These instructions will dictate a way of behaving that will change your life, perhaps to your detriment and perhaps to your benefit. Not knowing for sure where these instructions came from, and having no way of telling if they are really for you, you act on the instructions. Now what would you say about someone who took delivery of such a letter and acted in this way?

Q. *They are crazy!*

A. Yes, it would be very strange behavior wouldn't it? Yet you have no idea how thoughts appear in your mind, or where they come from. Despite this you take delivery of them, think they are personal to you, and you act on them. Does that make any sense to you?

Q. *I don't understand. Now I'm totally confused.*

A. That's great. Now, for a moment, your mind has stopped saying, "I know something," and is confused. Don't now try to make sense out of this confusion. It is the need to make sense, to give meaning that has got you in this mess in the first place. The delusion you have about yourself—as being an object—having personal control, is what keeps you struggling. You can never experience peace as long as this way of thinking persists. As long as you think you have personal control you will experience guilt, fear and anger when desires aren't met, and pride when they are. Either way you will experience limitation.

Q. *But when I feel guilt or anger I know how to transcend*

them and experience peace. I have a method of transcending such feelings.

A.   Who is transcending what?

Q.   *I am transcending those feelings and then I feel peace.*
A.   Let us say that you are able to transcend those feelings and feel peace. If you are really able to 'transcend,' why don't you just stay there, in peace?

Q.   *Well, I know that I am omnipresent, but I still have a body and it experiences those feelings. This is why I have learned to go into other dimensions. I know how to enter and go beyond the dimension of the senses into whole mind.*
A.   If, you are omnipresent then how, or why, would you transcend anything? Do you know what omnipresent means?

Q.   *No.*
A.   Omnipresent means everywhere. If you are everywhere, you are unlimited, so why do you care about experiences that happen through the limited body?

Q.   *Well, I still have a body, until I go to the other side.*

Q.   *(from another participant)...to the other side of omnipresence?*
A.   That you think you are omnipresent is an intellectual understanding only. Simply by saying, 'I am omnipresence,' you haven't stopped experiencing limitation and desires. You are still stuck in the idea that you are an object needing to affect other objects and affect yourself. If you are everything, then how come you care about 'others?' There can be no other if you are omnipresent, can there?

Q.   *But I do have a body and I am able to transcend it. I know how to astral travel and leave my body.*
A.   Who is leaving the body?

Q.   *I am.*

A. Who is this 'I' you are talking about?

Q. *You are confusing me.*
A. That is because you came here with rigid ideas about who you are. Each of them conflicting, but you've never thought them through. You think, 'I am omnipresent,' and still you want to help 'others.' You think, 'I am omnipresent,' and yet you think you can—and need to—transcend something.

All these ideas are experienced because you experience being. Without that experience no ideas would be perceived. You spend so much time priding yourself on all those ideas, even though you have no idea where they come from. You think of them as personal, even though it is clear they have all arisen despite you. All this knowledge keeps you ignorant of who you Really are.

Q. *But I know who I am.*
A. Who are you?

Q. *I know I am not the body, and that I am consciousness. I am able to go into various levels of consciousness, and various dimensions. When I do this I don't feel limited.*
A. When you close your eyes and simply experience being, can you locate that experience anywhere in your body? Can you isolate that experience, or limit it in any way?

Q. *No, I can't.*
A. As everyone has this exact same experience, when they close their eyes, doesn't it tell you, that consciousness is not limited in any way?

Q. *Yes.*
A. Then what is this about dimensions of consciousness? How can you compartmentalize something that is unlimited, without boundaries?

Q. *Well, I have various experiences. I go into one realm of consciousness and I feel peace. I go into the realm of the*

97

senses...

A.   Who is going into these realms? How could you experience
the idea of realms if you did not first experience being,
consciousness? All these experiences arise in consciousness,
but do not affect the experience of being in any way. You
may think, "Now I am being productive," or, "Now I am
being this or that," but you only experience any of this
because you Are—being. The sense 'I Am,' doesn't stop or
disappear, but you add onto it, 'I am this and that,' and
there the problems arise. It's because you think you are
some-thing that you are so concerned about the idea of
predestination. You want to know you will 'become' someone useful and that you have a purpose. This keeps you
goal-oriented, focused on, 'I Am like this,' and 'I want to
be like that.'

Q.   *I have never even thought of any of this. You are just*
sending my mind in circles.

A.   And that is all the mind ever does. It goes in circles, chasing
this concept then that. When it hits upon a concept it thinks
is important—or a truth—it latches onto it. Then the mind
is rather like a record with a stuck needle. It dwells on the
same idea on and on, until it latches onto a new and 'better' one. Think back over your life to all the different ideas
you have had. Each time, you thought, 'this is how it is,'
until the idea changed. How many times has a 'truth' been
invalidated in this way in your own experience?

Q.   *Now I just don't know what to think.*

A.   Good, don't even try. Do you know what the word real
means?

Q.   *Something that is. The world is real, the body is real.*

A.   An object changes, the body changes all the time. The word
real means, 'that which underlies appearances.' The word
relative pertains to 'significance in relation to other objects.'
An object is something that appears to you because you
experience being. The mind cannot understand how this
experience is possible. It can only think in terms of relativ-

98

ity (appearances) as being real (that which underlies appearances).

Q. *But the body is real. I experience it.*
A. How do you experience the body? You experience it because you are conscious. You experience it because you first experience 'I Am.' Without this primary experience, nothing could be experienced could it?

Q. *Well, no.*
A. Now listen again to what is being said. The mind thinks that relativity (appearances) is Reality (that which underlies appearances). The mind cannot think in any other way, because the mind's job is to conceptualize. It can only think that its concepts (appearances) are real (that which underlie appearances). If you understand this deeply you will realize that the mind can never know who you Really are.

Q. *I have just never asked any of these questions. They don't make any sense.*
A. No the mind can make no sense at all of who you Really are. The mind cannot know Reality because it is limited to concepts, appearances.

Q. *Then who am I?*
A. If something is constantly changing you cannot say it Is, you can only say it was and it might be. The body is constantly changing and one day it 'dies.' This means that it is not a constant. The body is an ever-changing appearance within a constant. That constant is the experience 'I Am.' If you want to know what is real you have to look at what is constant—essential—to the nature of an object. What is the only unchanging experience you have throughout your life? What experience do you have that is unaffected and unchanged, whether you are drunk, stoned, injured, upset?

Q. *(another participant) Breathing?*
A. If you have an asthma attack your breathing changes. If you smoke your breathing changes.

99

Q.   *(another participant) The experience of being alive.*

A.   Yes, the experience of being. That experience never ever disappears while the body is alive. That is the only constant you know, the experience 'I Am.'

Q.   *(another participant) In the movie* Cider House Rules, *the young man was a doctor and then he became an apple picker. Then he went back to being a doctor. Each time his job changed the experience, 'I Am,' didn't change.*

A.   Yes, that's right, the experience of being didn't stop. All that concerns you now is dis-identifying from 'I Am something,' and realizing You cannot be an ever-changing thing. When the experience of being ceases at the death of the body, does everyone else stop experiencing being?

Q.   *No.*

A.   When you close your eyes and experience being, you cannot locate it or limit in any way. As consciousness is the only constant, experienced by everyone as unlimited (when they close their eyes), don't you have to conclude that consciousness is all there is?

Q.   *Yes, I understand that all of this appears in consciousness.*

A.   Good. All of this is an appearance in consciousness. When a body is there consciousness is aware of itself and knows, 'I Am.' Consciousness expresses itself in unique ways through all the different bodyminds, yet underlying these varying expressions is still the sense 'I Am,' unchanged and unaffected. When the body dies there is no hole left in consciousness—it is omnipresent, everywhere. Consciousness then subsides into consciousness, so to speak, and is at rest. It hasn't disappeared, because all there is, Is consciousness.

Q.   *I don't get it. At one time I did everything to feel more alive, but then I kept on coming up against the idea of death. Death kept on confronting me.*

A.   Because the mind thinks you-the-body-mind is real, it is confronted by the termination of the body. But, you know you Are. You experience being and don't want this experience to end. Consciousness loves the experience of being. The mind loves the idea of immortality, but can only come to terms with the idea by means of concepts such as the soul migrating to another body and reincarnation. When you believe you are the body, you believe birth and death happen. But, the body is only experienced because of consciousness and when consciousness ceases being aware of itself in 'I Am,' it is at rest. Consciousness doesn't disappear because it has never appeared. Consciousness is all there is and you must Be That.

Q. *It is like trying to explain the color purple to a blind man.*
A. Yes exactly. The mind is like a blind man, only aware of concepts. To understand the Self, which is non-conceptual, is impossible for the mind.

Q. *This is so confusing.*
A. Good. That means that for a moment the mind is saying, 'I don't understand.' This is some progress because until now you thought you understood who you were. If you come here and gain new understandings that dilute old ones, that is helpful. What is not helpful is to latch onto them as any truth. Who you really are is beyond concepts, is non-conceptual, unnamable. How can you hope to understand the non-conceptual with the conceptualizing mind?

Q. *So, what can we do?*
A. There is nothing to do and nothing to avoid doing. The 'problem' is the need to understand and find meaning— concepts. If you want to know who you are, and understand You are not a concept, you will give up trying to know yourself by means of the conceptualizing mind. Or the mind may continue trying to understand, despite you, and that will just have to run its course. Either way, all you can do is continue living life, as you always have. There is nothing you can do with 'personal volition' to stop the delusion that the mind has created. This delusion happened

despite you, and can only cease despite you.

Q. *So is it like being at sea on a boat and not bothering to put the sails up or do anything?*

A. Thoughts, as you have agreed, happen despite you. These thoughts lead to actions, which must also happen despite you; because they are directed by impersonal thought. You have no say in whether you do or don't do anything. All actions happen despite you.

Q. *(another participant) Can you address the experience of being free of concepts?*

A. When all concepts are seen to be invalid, the mind is no longer split between thinking it is some-thing wanting to know its source. Then there is the clear apperception, or knowing, that you Are that source.

I know that I have a body that is unique to me and that I call mine, but I also know that I am not it. Concepts, thoughts, still arise in the mind, but they are not personalized in any way. This means that no thought is latched onto as holding any truth.

No action that happens is considered personal and therefore no action is judged. Thoughts are not censored and neither are actions. Everything is seen to occur spontaneously, despite the body. This means that there is absolutely no sense of guilt, no desires, and no ambitions or goals.

This doesn't mean that I sit around doing nothing. You try sitting around for two days doing nothing and in no time you'll find yourself doing something. If actions happen they happen, spontaneously and impersonally. I have no vested interest in acting a certain way, so actions happen efficiently. Actions are only inefficient when you judge them and effort to perform them just so. Why would I need to do anything in particular, and why would I need to avoid anything, unless it was harmful to someone else or to my body? Why would any experience be more or less important than any other?

All experiences are seen to be expressions happening through the body mind that is perceived in and by consciousness which I Am.

Q. *But you are still feeling the need to be here talking with us.*
A. I feel no need at all. I have no vested interest in giving these talks or in their outcome. I don't care if you 'get' what is being said or not.

Satsangs were requested and at first the thought came, 'Now that I am no longer a miserable seeker, why on earth do I want to be surrounded by them?" The mind made a judgment, but it wasn't pursued or rejected. Satsang began to happen, but I would be just as happy at home cleaning the floors, or playing with my dogs. Either experience is just an experience. I don't have a need for any particular experience because I Am unaffected by any experience. I know that I am consciousness in which this whole play of experiences happens, and is perceived via this body. When the body is dead, nothing will have 'happened' to Me. I was never born and will never die.

Q. *Thank you.*
A. Now perhaps you have understood something, but it is merely an understanding, not a knowing, not an experiencing. Don't latch onto anything that has been said here. You may ponder what has been said, but recognize that the mind is still trying to understand. Remember that conceptualizing is what got you into this mess of thinking you are a thing with personal willpower. If trying to understand happens, it happens despite you, so don't get mad with the mind. Gradually the mind will tire of all this.

In the *Crest Jewel of Discrimination* it is put so well (paraphrased). If you are sick, simply saying the word, "Medicine' will not make you get better. If you want to be the king of a country, simply saying, "I am king," will not mean you are going to suddenly find yourself ruling as king. Simply by saying, "I am omnipresenct," or, "I am not the body or mind," does not mean you are going to lose identification with those concepts.

If you know there is a buried treasure and you want it, just saying, "Come forth," isn't going to make it appear. Similarly, the Self is like buried treasure, buried beneath all your concepts. Simply by saying, "I am not the bodymind," will not make the identification with the bodymind disappear.

All you can do is what you are doing. It has always been this way. The deeper this understanding goes, the less sense the idea of personal control will make. Then, gradually, judgment of thoughts and actions will diminish. There is nothing you can do to speed this up or slow it down. You can only Be as you Are. All this has happened despite you, and it can only cease despite you.

Q. *But, how do we know what are natural, spontaneous actions as compared to efforts?*

A. When an action happens and you think of it as a personal effort you don't experience peace. This is because you are judging it, judging the outcome, and judging how others will perceive you.

Even if your body is straining because of an action, but you feel peaceful, that action is natural. If an emotion arises, such as grief or anger, and you experience it fully, without censorship, you will discover that it is underlain by peace. You have experience of this when you say, "I just love being around my friend because I can let it all hang out, act grumpy, act moody, and she doesn't judge me. When I'm with her I can just be myself." Right there, in that expression of 'being myself,' you have your answer. When you are not judging or expecting to be judged, you can 'be yourself' and there is peace.

You don't need to explore which personality traits are natural to you and which are not. After a lifetime of living via a contrived personality, it is often very hard to distinguish what is natural to you. You simply need to recognize that uncensored actions are underlain by peace. Emotions and experiences that are fully experienced, without judgment, are underlain by peace. Peace is your essential nature and so it is never absent, merely obscured by judgment and censorship.

Q. *I see.*
A. When you experience peace do you ask, "Why is this happening or how long will it last?" Clearly, the thoughts usually arise at some point, because the mind is used to thinking of peace as a luxury. But until those thoughts arise you don't do anything to change what is being experienced do you? Who you are is essentially peaceful and the only reason you don't experience this all the time is because you think, 'I Am some-one' needing to be a certain way. It is simply a matter of finding out who you are not.

Beneath all the facades is the treasure, the Self, unaffected by anything. You have glimpses of your essential nature all the time, yet you continue to feel you need to become other than you are. The one you think is in need of changing is unreal. This person is a figment of your imagination, a character you have become so used to playing out that you think it Is you. You are like a method actor who has immersed himself so fully, and stayed so long in character, he no longer remembers who he was before the play began.

Who you really are has been sitting in the audience all along, witnessing this play. Right now you are involved in strutting around on the stage of life, desiring applause and dreading rejection. When you find out who you are not all, that will cease.

When Satsang was over, the predominant questioner came to me. What he said was a clear indication that he had come with an agenda, very strongly believing that a personal concept was important. In such cases, the mind veils everything that it hears with its own accumulation of knowledge.

Rather than coming, hoping to gain relief from rigid thinking, the questioner spends all his time comparing his concepts to those being presented. Then, no concept can percolate beyond the mind because the heart is under such strong censorship. Nevertheless, when confusion is felt, as in this case, it is also a sign that the rigidity of existing concepts is perhaps ready to become more flexible.

Q. *I have developed a method to help people experience peace. I have found that when they do this technique it causes spontaneous healing. I am like you, I experience peace all the time, underlying everything. I teach much along the same lines you do.*

A. If your constant experience is of peace why do you have any desires?

Q. *I don't. I just want to help people while I am here in a body.*

A. To want is to desire. If you want to help people it is because you think something needs changing. When peace is the constant, underlying experience, where is the need to change anything? What is, as it is, is experienced fully and whatever the experience, peace underlies it.

I am not giving you a contrived way of 'causing' the experience of peace. I am telling you that peace is your essential nature. As long as there are desires to change what is, peace is not a constant experience. What you are saying is that you personally cause the experience of peace and that this experience will cause spontaneous healing.

In contrived actions there is no real peace, because you think of them as happening through personal effort. How can effort and peace co-exist? When you understand that everything happens despite you, then true healing happens. This healing is of the split mind, torn between this desire and that, needing to change, censor and 'fix.'

Your essential nature is peaceful, is peace. Now find out why that is not your constant experience. Whatever you say, if you still need to, 'go into dimensions of consciousness' in order to change experiences, then clearly peace doesn't underlie them. That is, you are unaware of the peace that is always there because it is natural to you.

Desires, goals, and the need to 'fix' will always keep you ignorant of your essential nature. Find out who is experiencing these desires. How is the knowing of these desires happening and to whom? Find out who you re not, then, maybe the knowing of who you Are will become apparent.

I *went everywhere with longing*
In my eyes, until here
In my own house
I felt truth
Filling my sight.

NAKED SONG, LALLA
(*Translation by*
Coleman Barks)

Pain and Suffering

People frequently ask me why there is pain and suffering in the world. Firstly I would suggest that questions about what is happening in the world are mere distractions. The real 'problem' is what you consider personal pain and personal suffering.

If you didn't consider pain and suffering personal, you wouldn't care what was happening in the world. This sounds harsh, but think of a time when you were totally contented and at peace. Did you worry about the world? Probably you were more inclined to see the positive, uplifting images the world presented you.

The cares you have about the world are worries and have nothing to do with the heart. When you feel bad you project your feelings outward, so as to distract yourself. The world is just a reflection of your own attitudes.

As long as your mind is full of value judgments about good, bad, right, and wrong, you suffer. As long as you want only good feelings you are in a constant mode of struggle.

What constitutes right and wrong in your mind is rarely a universal paradigm. If everyone put down on paper their view of what world peace would look like, you would have millions of different views. This means that if your view of world peace were to materialize, not everyone would experience it as peaceful.

If you look back over your life, you will see that your attitudes have changed frequently. What once seemed acceptable and valid suddenly made no sense to you. Then as you grew older you may have readopted your initial beliefs. Each time you held a thought about 'this is how it is' you felt it was absolutely right.

Looking back over your life, you realize that your own personal absolutes have changed frequently. Your idea of what would constitute world peace today is probably very different to the image you would have had of it as a teenager. "No discipline, no work, no curfews." This also tells you that all judgments are illusory—impermanent.

The desire for peace and an end to suffering and pain in the world is a reflection of your own attitudes. You suffer because of these attitudes, not because of what is going on in the world. External suffering simply reminds you of your own personal pains. Rather than dealing with them, it is much easier to distract yourself in 'fixing' everything— and everyone— around you.

When you were a tiny infant your mind wasn't full of judgments about good and bad. Pain may have been there, but you didn't think, "I have to stop this." Actions such as crying, laughing, and even struggling, happened spontaneously. Despite physical discomfort, the newborn infant just Is, with no judgments about anything. There, within struggle and pain, the infant still experiences peace of mind. The peace wasn't caused by the mind, but by the absence of rigid judgments. This peace underlies anything that might be happening to the child or in its environment.

When judgments fill the mind, peace is a foreign experience to you. If you understand this you will understand that circumstances are not the cause of what you feel. Your beliefs and attitudes determine what and how you feel. As Ramesh wrote in one of his books, "Thoughts are the tension." What he was talking about is involvement with thoughts.

The reason the jnani experiences peace is because there is no involvement. He or she is not identified with any experience and doesn't think of any experience as personal. If the jnani is injured, there is pain—perhaps tremendous pain—but it is merely experienced. The jnani may take practical steps, such as taking a painkiller, but he does not NEED anything to change. All experiences are witnessed impersonally when they arise, and the subsiding of them is also an impersonal occurrence.

The jnani doesn't care about anything. That is, there is no worry, no involvement, no need to change anything. What happens happens, and if practical steps are taken to change something, these actions are not fuelled by worry or need.

It is a myth that the jnani only experiences peace. Because the jnani still has a body that interacts with other bodies, he or she still experiences all the vicissitudes of life. Yes, there is only peace underlying all experiences, but this doesn't mean that pain, suffering, and strong emotions, don't arise.

Because there is no need to censor anything, everything is experienced fully. Just imagine experiencing pain, anger, or grieving fully. You have probably never done this because your mind is always at the ready, trying to stop what it doesn't like.

When the mind is not involved in rejecting and clinging, nothing matters. There isn't any need to change what is, as it is. Physical and emotional pain and suffering aren't the 'problem' you are concerned with. The problem is your attitude about it.

I recall, when judgment and censorship first fell away, there were those who seemed to watch my every move. If anger arose they would raise their eyebrows and question why. If grieving happened, they couldn't understand it's intensity. "Why do you react even more strongly now, if you are not identified with anything? It sure looks as if you are involved!"

It is the mind's nature to react and the jnani still has a functioning mind. If a loved one dies, grieving happens. If someone kills my dog, anger will probably arise. Sometimes it looks as if there is involvement because thoughts about a situation arise in quick succession. Then corresponding emotions also arise in quick succession. Outwardly it may look as if there is an over-reaction. What is happening is that thoughts and emotions arise, but are not pursued. The quick succession of uncensored thoughts shows itself in uncensored emotions. Externally it may appear as if there is involvement, but all there is Is uncensored—deep and full experiencing.

If you are craving 'enlightenment' because you think it means an end to emotional ups and downs, think again. The jnani isn't a vegetable that no longer experiences emotions. The jnani simply Knows that no experience is personal and so there is no instinct to censor any experience.

When you don't take things personally, you know that emotions can still arise. You watch a romantic movie, all the while knowing it is just a story and not real, but you cry. When the movie is over you might even say, "I love a good cry." Have you ever wondered why horror movies are so popular? It's because people know they are not real, and so it gives them an arena in which they can experience extreme fear fully.

Intuitively you recognize that to fully experience an emotion, whatever it may be, feels good. This is because it makes you feel alive. You don't think about it in these terms perhaps, but when emotions are allowed to be fully felt, you feel more vital than ever. If you pay attention at such times you will recognize that, underlying the emotion, there is peace. This peace is because censorship is absent.

The jnani Knows that the ever-changing images the world presents are not Real. He Knows that no circumstance affects or changes who he Is in any way. So why reject or cling to anything? Why care about anything being a certain way?

It's only because you take everything personally that you struggle to understand why there is pain and suffering. If I told you 'why' these experiences exist, would it make them any easier for you to bear? You might think, "Yes, if I knew the reason I could cope with them better."

This is precisely what you would do—you would cope. Nothing would have changed, because you are always just coping. You aren't dealing head on or fully with anything.

So often on TV we hear stories about people being rescued from drowning or similar dangers. The rescuer will often say things such as, "I didn't think twice. I just jumped in and did what needed doing." They didn't stand there thinking, "I wonder why this is happening." "I wonder what I should do." They acted, practically, efficiently, and with no mental involvement. They didn't take action while wondering, "I wonder if I will succeed."

When the need to understand is absent, actions are always efficient and practical. If someone jumps into raging waters to save another person, you will probably describe them as caring. This is a very different caring to the worrying kind you are talking about when you, 'care about the state of the world.'

The jnani cares about nothing, and is totally present to all happenings. You care about everything and are totally self-involved. You may think caring about starving children in Ethiopia describes altruism. If your mind is judging and asking questions about this situation it isn't an indication of altruism. It signifies that you are involved in needing to change what is, because you think it is 'bad.'

When I see suffering going on in the world, thoughts still arise about it. The mind hasn't stopped judging because this is its job. The difference is that no thought is pursued or dwelt on. Judgments arise, but they subside with equal ease. If the thought to take a certain action arises, the action may happen and it may not. If steps are taken to deal with anything, there is no thought of outcome.

Planning still happens, but there is no need for any particular results. If I arrange a plane flight and it's cancelled, the thought may arise, "Bummer, now I'm going to be late." This thought isn't pursued and no worry arises. Practical steps are taken to deal with what is, as it is. The circumstances are not ideal, but no thoughts existed as to ideals in the first place.

I would prefer to live in a comfortable home, surrounded by my family and animals. If I had to live on the streets this would be less comfortable, but it would be experienced for what it is—a new experience.

If you live in the world experiencing everything that presents itself fully, no experience needs avoiding. Actually, to experience fully eliminates the possibility of avoiding.

It is only because you judge some experiences bad and some good that you do not Know constant underlying peace. While you are rejecting and clinging—that is all you know; the struggle between one judgment and another.

While you are 'caring' about the state of the world, or your own state, the mind is split between what it wants and what is not. Meanwhile, what Is is experienced through distorted mental filters.

See, feel, touch, taste, and listen, fully and there is no opportunity for judgment to get in the way. Judgments may still arise, but there will be no time to embellish on them because you are fully present—Being.

Discover why you need to change what is. Explore why you

want things to be a certain way. Is it because you 'care' so much about others, or is it because YOU don't like the feelings you are having?

Where 'caring' and fearing is, altruism is not. When 'caring,' fearing, and the need to 'fix' is happening, peace is absent. The only suffering that really concerns you is the suffering that is happening in your own mind. Be clear on this and stop distracting yourself with 'others.'

This may sound like a recipe for selfishness, but selfishness is just another judgment. It describes doing what you want with disregard for others. I'm not saying disregard others, I am suggesting that you look at the attitudes you have about them.

If you have any strong ideas about anyone it doesn't change 'them.' You may feel good if you are with someone you think is 'really nice.' You may feel bad if you are around someone you judge 'horrible.' Other people don't cause these feelings, your attitudes about them do.

Investigate what you think is important, such as 'an end to suffering,' 'an end to poverty,' 'an end to struggle.' Ask yourself why these concepts are so important to you. You will find that they are 'important' because they give you trains of thought to pursue that 'fill the void.'

What is not understood is that this 'void' is empty of concepts. This means that it is beyond the conceptual self and precisely the 'place' the seeker is—usually misguidedly—aiming for.

While you are aiming for peace you are focused toward what is not and how you want it to be. These "thoughts are the tension" that keep you obsessed with what seems lacking. Meanwhile, you experience what Is through the distorting filters of your fears and desires.

All these words are so well summed up by Kris Kristofferson. "Freedom's just another word for nothin' left to lose." Stop trying to understand. Be fully with what is, and there You are.

Until you realize that no experience is more or less
important than any other, diversity will be
blamed as the cause of adversity.

Where are the boundaries now?
What was that strange dream
That kept me locked in sleep?
At last I open my eyes
And know that sleep was nothing more
Than the space between You and me
In which I searched for both.
Until the nightmare awakened me
To that same space
That is no space at all.
Nothing but Self
What miracle this place
Without location.

E.V.

Depression and the need to control

Depression falls under a multitude of categories and appears to be triggered by various factors. Food and chemical intolerances, genetic disposition, and circumstance may appear to be possible causes. Depression can present itself in ecstatic highs and the deepest 'lows.'

My focus here is not to investigate the cause or various forms of depression with you. What I will be addressing are common elements that accompany most forms of this dis-ease.

For people who don't suffer from overt depression, it's often hard to relate to those who do. They can't understand why such people can't just 'pull' themselves out of it. They look at these seemingly successful people and find it impossible to understand how or why they cannot simply appreciate what they have.

One of the Latin translations of depression is *animus fractus,* which signifies the 'split,' or broken mind. This translation best describes the dis-ease. However, it doesn't just describe clinical depression, but also the state of mind of *anyone* who is identified with the body-object and the multifaceted false personality.

From this perspective most *everyone* can be said to be in a continual state of depression. So if you think this chapter doesn't apply to you, think again. As long as your mind is focused on extremes—wanting this versus that—it is 'split.' While this 'split' persists, you de-press (shove down) 'bad' feelings and try to maintain the 'good' ones. This describes a state of dis-ease and also the state of de-pression.

It may be helpful to note here that I am not writing a hypothesis on depression. During my lifetime I experienced frequent and severe bouts of it—beginning at a very early age. The two experiences that best described these times were 'overwhelm' and 'feeling out of control.' It is these two perceptions that I will be addressing here.

During your lifetime you have probably enjoyed certain times when you felt 'out of control.' During sexual intimacy, when such abandon happens, the feelings can be wonderful. When you first fall in love, the lack of control can feel liberating.

During your lifetime you have probably also experienced the pain of feeling 'out of control.' At such times everything overwhelms you, and all you want is some order, or self-discipline, or better finances. This tells you that 'being out of control' has two forms.

If you throw caution to the wind deliberately, your resulting emotions are often dictated by the outcome. Sometimes, 'just for the heck of it,' you take a gamble and act spontaneously knowing that, 'I'll probably pay for this later.' Other times you do everything possible to empower yourself and control still slips through your fingers.

Thus, control appears to be both a personal choice and something you have no power over. Strangely, few people question the obviousness of this paradox.

If you look at your life honestly you will probably see that this dynamic is always at play. You enjoy control when you have it, and enjoy the feelings that arise when you 'choose' to abandon it. Then, you lament the inexplicable 'loss' when control vanishes.

The seeming ability to reject this and embrace that gives you the idea you have personal power and that control is real. IF this were true, why is it that sometimes, despite all your efforts, you 'lose' control totally?

For something to be considered real it has to be unchanging. If control is sometimes your experience and other times not, you have to conclude that it is an invalid concept. The trouble is that the mind is 'split' because of the belief that contradictory concepts, such as good and bad are unrelated.

Control wouldn't be considered necessary unless its opposite, lack of control, existed in-potential within it. Intuiting this potential gives rise to expectation of it, and this is what keeps life seeming like one big struggle.

Life describes constant change, manifesting in oscillations between positive and negative. The need to avoid and control change signifies rejection of life.

Note that I am not talking about the initiation of practical steps to effect change. I am referring to needy, fear-engendered actions that require, at all odds, a specific outcome. While actions are fuelled by fear, guilt, and desire, they are never practical. Usually such actions are un-centered and inefficient because all your focus is on results rather than what you are doing.

Unless results are pleasing, life remains un-enjoyable. What is, is never sufficiently fulfilling, and what is not always seems to be a better alternative. This describes an insidious form of depression, but 'hope' is a wonderful way of coping and avoiding experiencing it fully.

When clinical depression results, for whatever seeming reason, it is a time when you lose the 'strength' to hold up all your facades. This is when people yearn to just 'be my old self' again. They find themselves thinking, 'I just don't know who I am anymore.'

What is happening is that suddenly the unknown is being faced. Until that moment, the pseudo-persona was their orientation to the world. When it disappears, they find themselves feeling 'empty' and lost.

In New-age thinking, people now look at disruptive times in their life as an opportunity to learn something about themselves. The trouble is, this paradigm often stops people from fully experiencing what is. They are so busy analyzing it, that the analysis itself becomes a coping mechanism.

When the deep 'lows' of depression hit, the mind is incapable of analysis. It just doesn't seem to function properly and all there seems to be is the 'tunnel' and you. What I am about to propose is not a form of analysis or coping.

When the 'tunnels' hit, they force you beyond your comfort zone. Your comfort zone is the false persona because you are very familiar with it—even if it frustrates you. When this is absent you feel lost and incapable of enjoying or feeling anything.

However frequently you may suffer from depression, this absence of feelings and identity feels unnatural. This means that you are more familiar with being 'a certain way.' Because clinical depression is considered a disease, you conclude that your 'natural' state is the pseudo-personality.

Many doctors, psychologists, and laypeople are all too quick to conclude that the motivated personality is healthy. Motivation requires external input, goal-orientation, and the desire to succeed. This pretty much defines the makeup of the false 'you'— always needing to be-come other than you are.

The word inspiration comes from the Greek, meaning 'to be filled with the spirit.' Enthusiasm is also a word rooted in the Greek language, and means 'to be filled with God.' Enthusiasm and inspiration may sometimes be the result of motivation. More often than not, however, they seem to 'come out of the blue' and just take over.

You never talk of 'needing to get enthused,' but motivation is always accompanied by need. You sigh and tell yourself, "I have to get motivated." This gives you an indication that motivation is not natural to you, but is contrived.

Because the so-called 'depressive' totally lacks motivation they are considered ill. Clearly they don't feel inspired either, but this is because they are used to focusing on the 'me,' thinking 'it' is what gets inspired.

If you observe the times you felt inspired, it is always then that you 'lose yourself' in whatever you are doing. This means that inspiration happens despite *the 'me' identity.*

If you recognize that the personalized 'me' is a dis-ease state, when it falls away—as in depression—you might say you are actually healthier. Of course, the body is often undergoing a chemical imbalance, so you may refute this idea—especially if you are a doctor.

As an example, 'enlightenment' describes the falling away of the 'me.' Once this 'falling away' is irreversible, the body becomes increasingly vital and healthy. If cancer or any other disease was in-potential in that body prior to this 'happening' it may still result. But the general physical makeup is far healthier, so it deals with disease in a much more dynamic way.

In the initial stages of 'enlightenment' the falling away process of the 'me' is invariably experienced as depression. Often the words 'dark night of the soul' are used instead, but this doesn't make matters feel any better. Depression is still the experience.

Whether you experience classical depression, or what is termed the 'dark night of the soul,' it means the 'me' has lost its strength. If you understand this dynamic clearly, the emptiness that is experienced can be dealt with in a constructive way.

Struggle may still result, but if you watch the struggle you will realize you are separate to it. To observe anything you have to be separate to it—this is plain logic. If you observe the feeling of emptiness deeply, you will again discover that you are separate to this emptiness.

The ability to control is not something you experience when depression hits. When you find yourself feeling 'out of control' or 'overwhelmed,' observe these experiences too. Again, you will realize that you are separate to them.

Whether you struggle to control, or struggle to stop trying to control, you end up with struggle. If you observe the battle to control, rather than letting it overwhelm you, gradually you realize that you are also separate to it.

This is not a prescription for 'curing' depression. Neither is it a prescription for coping with, or avoiding your experience. On the contrary, this is a description of how to stay fully present to what is going on.

Depression is one of the singularly most out of control experiences in a lifetime. As such, it offers the greatest opportunity for understanding why *who you THINK you are*, desires control. Depression can give you deep insight into the existential dilemma of desiring what is not.

At first it is not easy to stay present while trying to resist or control. But, each time it happens, the habit of controlling dissolves somewhat. By staying present I am not referring to coping or 'being detached.' Staying present means staying in non-involvement.

You may wonder how struggle and non-involvement can be possible simultaneously. Understand that the idea of control only arises because of the concept of lack of control. Involvement or struggle signifies rejecting what is. Non-involvement means being present to what is. To stay present to involvement, or remain uninvolved in involvement, is not as strange as it seems.

The 'me' identity is a sum of all 'your' desires and needs. Desires and needs are synonymous with control. When what Is satisfies you no desires arise, and so the act of controlling is also absent. Who you Really are is obscured by the needy 'me' identity. This means that who you Really are cannot be realized until the concept of control is recognized as an illusion.

At the time of the deepest 'lows' even emotions do not happen. All you care about is that you cannot 'care' about anything. Depression is always accompanied by the deepest apathy—not feeling or caring.

If you realize that caring much of the time includes worry, then apathy means the absence of worry. When I first realized this during depression, it actually set me laughing. There I was, trying to care, and suddenly discovering the absence of caring wasn't such a bad thing after all.

A more explicit word to describe this experience is dispassion. Dispassion means impartiality or neutrality. If you observe the emptiness you feel—rather than trying to figure it out—you will discover that it is neutral.

Because the 'me' is anything but neutral it finds this emptiness terrifying. Depression seems like an extreme state, but if you understand that it actually gives you a respite from swinging between extremes your whole paradigm begins to change.

Bi-polar disorders are a swinging between extreme. The experiences can vary, but often the person swings between ecstatic highs and deep lows. During the deep lows, the process of observing is still possible.

Depression will not necessarily cease because of this. You will not lose the 'me' identity and become 'enlightened' either. What can happen, albeit gradually, is that you begin facing clinical depression and the ups and downs of life with a new perspective.

It's easy when you are a 'seeker' to fixate on the idea that life will never be fulfilling unless you 'attain.' This notion keeps you avoiding life as is, which is the habit of the pseudo 'you.' If you understand this, you will also recognize that by fixating on what is not (enlightenment), you are strengthening the very 'me' you want to see beyond.

To stay present to what 'Is' and experiencing it *fully,* means both the negative and positive aspects of it—you have to 'lose yourself' in whatever is happening. That is, you can't be focused on the past, or the future.

In day-to-day living it's very easy to stay distracted and entertain the 'me' with fancies about the future. The extreme times of your life, however, are ones that afford you no opportunity for such distractions.

Whether you are grieving the loss of a loved one, experiencing depression, fear, or in the first throws of falling in love, these are 'extreme' times. Recognize that during them your facades—temporarily—fall away.

When the 'me' subsides, however temporarily and for whatever reason, these are the easiest times to be fully with what is. For sure, when you are deeply in love, this is the most enjoyable form of being present. But, if you observe *any* extreme experience, be it fear, grief, or joy, you will see that the experience of it consumes you totally.

At such times, whatever the experience, it is underlain by peace, because nothing is being avoided. You are unable to be distracted by anything.

You don't need to 'wait for enlightenment' or a better day, or a windfall, in order to experience underlying peace. It is your essential nature and you have glimpses of it all the time. These glimpses happen particularly in the worst times, IF you pay attention.

There you have been, most of your life, waiting for life to be perfect. Meanwhile the goal-oriented 'me' blinds you to the fact that even the seemingly worst experiences are underlain by Perfection.

Satsang: The Struggle for Peace

At the beginning of satsang I asked the regular participants why they continued visiting each week.

Q. *I feel so peaceful when I'm here. There isn't anywhere else I could be or want to be.*

A. What happens to you between the times you are here?

Q. *I have begun noticing that I am less reactionary. Situations occur which would normally agitate me, but I find myself not caring.*

A. It's good you notice this, but is this diminishment in involvement considered a personal experience?

Q. *Yes, it's still considered personal.*

A. Just don't fall into the trap of thinking 'you' have made progress. It's fine to enjoy the changes, but you must be careful not to latch onto them, or take pride in them.

Q. *(another participant) I am like the Energizer Bunny. When I come here I feel peaceful, and in between that peace keeps on going and going until the next time. I come here to 'recharge my battery.' (laughing)*

A. As long as you think I am causing that peace, you'll keep on returning. What you need to ask is, "How is experiencing of this peace possible?"

Q. *Because 'I Am.'*

A.   How is the knowing 'I Am,' possible? To whom is this knowing happening? These are the questions you must ask.

Q.   *Can you talk more about interaction and involvement?*
A.   When one pseudo-identity is with another, the reflection of these two personalities bounce off each other. Whether attraction or repulsion occurs, there's involvement. Each is involved in projecting himself, or herself, onto the other. Both personalities desire either to create a bond or to cause antagonism.

Whatever the purpose, it is motivated by the idea that there is real separation between a 'me' and the 'other.' This delusion of separateness gives rise to the need to control that which is seen as separate to the self. That means you are constantly in a mode of trying to manipulate life.

The word *involve* means: to cause, to share, or participate, in an experience. While the idea of causation exists, it is because actions are thought of as personal. As long as personal volition is believed possible, you can't help but think in terms of others *making* you feel. While you hold this belief, you're not free of the idea that 'you' can *make* others feel.

This mode of thinking is very evident in our language. On a daily basis, people say, "It made me feel," "she made me feel," "I make him feel." When you use such words, what you're essentially conveying is that individuals have power over each other's emotions. This line of thinking is what is called victim-consciousness.

Q.   *But I feel such strong feelings when I am in your presence.*
A.   When you sit in front of me there is no pseudo-identity mirroring yours. What you feel is the absence of presence. The relief of this calms the mind and you feel centered.

It's this rare experience of centeredness in yourself that you feel. You are glimpsing 'I Am' without the labels. This gives you a sense of presence you aren't used to having, so you project that presence onto me. You attribute an-other with how you feel—and that's the old habit—but there is no 'other.'

Q. *I see.*

A. The habit of believing 'others' are the cause of how you feel, kicks in, and then it's easy to make me—and coming here, a crutch.

While you're in satsang you feel peaceful. Between visits you may remain lulled by the knowledge that you'll soon be able to 'recharge' yourself with another visit.

While you're in satsang, the mind calms and peace is felt. Temporarily the habit of involvement—'causing' another to feel a certain way—is dispelled. You are happy to sit here in an arena where no 'other' requires anything of you.

If you find that reactionary behavior is diminishing and actions are more spontaneous, clearly this is a benefit. However, if you go away thinking your visits are helping you 'gain' peace you are personalizing that experience.

Q. *So what is the difference in your sense of peace?*

A. Peace is a deceptive word, because in general terms it means the absence of strife. The 'peace beyond all understanding' that describes 'enlightenment' contains no concepts at all—not even enlightenment.

There is no thought of freedom, because the concept of limitation isn't recognized. There is no attachment to peace because the concept of strife is absent.

This impersonal peace is better understood by means of the word neutrality. That is, there's total dispassion - impartiality. Your mind can't conceive of neutrality because it's locked into dualistic thinking. Either there is peace or there is strife. Either there is freedom or there is limitation.

If you browse through a dictionary, you'll find that many words are explained by means of their counterpart. For example, silence is explained as 'lack of noise;' peace as the 'absence of strife.'

It doesn't take much logic to recognize that no concept can exist without its opposite. The minute you think of virtue, you are acknowledging the existence of sin. The minute you think of good, you are acknowledging the existence of bad.

While the mind thinks dualistically, it's always engaged in rejecting one concept for the sake of another. It doesn't recognize that no concept can exist without its contradiction, in-potential within it. The logic the mind prides itself on is really blind logic.

Q. *You mentioned jnana yoga. Can you explain it again?*
A. The 'path' of jnana yoga is the investigation of concepts. It's really what we have just been talking about. It's the investigating of the meaning of words as opposed to their connotations. It's the investigation of each concept and its contradiction. The ultimate purpose is to deeply realize that no concept is an absolute. All concepts contain their counterpart in-potential within them.

Superficially, the mind 'gets' this pretty quickly once you've begun. But, it keeps on being tripped up by concepts. It's a whole unraveling process because the mind has been tied up in knots all your life.

When the paradox of language and life is deeply realized, the mind gives up looking for absolutes. This includes the search for the Self. The mind, realizing it can never know an absolute, acknowledges that it can never understand who you Really are. When the mind totally gives up trying to understand, in that moment, the non-conceptual Self is 'realized.'

Q. *So what you teach in Breakthrough is really jnana yoga.*
A. Yes, but when I was evolving Breakthrough I had no idea that the process had a name. I'd never heard of jnana yoga.

But do understand that nothing 'you' do can *cause* anything to happen. It doesn't matter if you do jnana yoga, stand on your head or become a fruitarian, it's all just Consciousness at play. If something happens it just happens. It might *seem* as if 'your' actions were the cause. But, you've never had any say in any happening.

Q. *It's so hard to really 'get' that even though, intellectually, I feel I understand it.*

A. Only when you stop thinking you understand *anything* will you 'get' it.

Jnana yoga isn't *necessary*, but if it happens it happens. The trouble is the mind wants to 'do' something. Most disciplines risk boosting the ego by giving the sense 'I Am making progress,' when the discipline is adhered to.

IF you do jnana yoga, it doesn't feel like a discipline. It's more like an obsession. The mind becomes obsessed with deconstructing concepts. This means that it's actually trying to deconstruct itself.

The idea of 'progress' is the antithesis of jnana yoga because it's about involution, not evolution. This is why it's the most constructive 'path' because, paradoxically, it's all about de-construction. The ego doesn't have a hope of puffing itself up in that kind of process. It's all about deconstructing the idea that control is real.

Q. *And we can't control the need to control.*

A. No, of course not. The idea of personal control arose despite you. So, how do you think 'you' can control it? What you can do is investigate the root of the 'problem'— desires. By replacing one addiction, one involvement, for another you don't transcend involvement. What you need to ask is, "who is addicted to addiction?" "Who is involved with involvement?" "How is the experiencing of all this possible?"

Q. *But if we're feeling peace from coming here, that has to be a positive sign too doesn't it?*

A.   The peace I talk of is neutrality. When there is neutrality there is total absence of involvement. Neutrality is not dependant on circumstance, because, by definition, it doesn't contain the element of comparing.

Recognize that here you have the possibility of experiencing non-involvement. This experience brings a sense of peace to the personality you are identified with. If you see this peace as just a respite from your reactionary personality, you won't latch onto it. You can still enjoy it, but don't consider it a measure of progress. All that's happened is that you are able to experience a degree of impartiality where usually involvement is strong. The experience of peace you have isn't impartiality. It's still a personal experience as long as you are identified with all your labels.

Unless all concepts have fallen away, your investigation of self must continue. There are no levels of progress and no degrees of enlightenment. Either you know, beyond a shadow of a doubt, that you are not a concept, or you are identified with a concept.

Only when peace is experienced as absolute neutrality, can it be called 'the peace beyond all understanding.' While you covet peace, it is because you are involved with the idea of strife.

I'm not 'in a state of peace.' States of consciousness are only relative experiences. They are constantly changing, and one minute you feel peaceful, the next you feel agitated.

I am beyond 'states,' because I am That, which precedes relative states.

Q.   *But how can I realize that I am not what I experience myself to be?*

A.   The word 'realization' perpetuates the idea that some-one, namely you-the-pseudo-personality, can know Reality. Clearly an appearance cannot know, or Be, that within which it appears.

As a dualistic concept cannot know the undifferentiated Self, no-one ever Self-realizes. This expression just differentiates between one who believes himself to be an object and 'one' who is no longer identified with any concepts.

When I talk of all concepts 'falling away,' I mean that all concepts are seen to be unreal. That which perceives this faulty perception cannot Be, and has never been a concept. You can only Be That which is prior to all conceptualization.

Until this knowing is total, don't let the mind lull you into thinking peaceful feelings are significant. They may be enjoyable, but if they are dependant on circumstance they are only of relative significance. That is they give you respite from your usual jostling between desiring this and rejecting that.

Until all concepts are recognized as unreal, the knowing of who you Are cannot happen. The unreal 'you,' with all the labels, can never know the Real you.

Q.   *Since I've been coming here I feel as if a lot of labels have fallen away.*

A.   It's good that you probably have more perspective on your labels. IF a lot of labels had fallen away, you would probably not be experiencing the peace you say you feel.

You'd probably be sitting there feeling like Mary.

You see, the labels have been your identity all your life. When they really begin to fall away, the experience is painful. Usually there is a deep sense of emptiness and often depression.

Q.   *(participant I am talking about) Yes I feel so empty and seem to cry all the time. At the same time it's a kind of relief. It's strange.*

A.   Yes, because you have an understanding of what is happening there's relief. The 'trick' is not to try filling that emptiness.

Q. *I don't even seem to be able to do that. It's just over whelming.*

A. But if you think about what filled the emptiness, isn't that overwhelming? The pseudo-personality is always on alert, always needing to control everything. That was pretty exhausting and overwhelming wasn't it?

Q. *Yes. It's almost as if there's peace and struggle happening at the same time.*

A. As long as labels remain, the mind is still 'split' and will struggle with the emptiness. All you can do is sit in-between the peace and struggle and ride it out. Actually, peace is your essential nature, so it underlies this struggle. Peace has always been there because it's natural to you.

As the emptiness 'grows' struggle subsides too. And during all this there can be times of just feeling in limbo.

Q. *Yes, that's exactly how it feels - limbo.*

A. It may have seemed better to know 'this is how it is,' but now all your certainties about who you are are collapsing. This can be terrifying, but at least you know to some degree who you are NOT.

Q. *Yes.*

Q. *(another participant) So what you're saying is that this process is always a painful one.*

A. Yes, it does seem that in all cases pain is inevitable. How many of your life transitions have been painless? Growing up, puberty, marriage, moving house, changing jobs— haven't most of these life transitions incurred some distress and pain?

Q. *Yes, most of them.*

A. Do you really think the transformation of your being from a pseudo identity to knowing Self is going to be any less painful?

Believing you are the false personality, with all its needs

and guilt, is painful. The trouble is most people have become so good at coping and covering up this pain they aren't even conscious of it.

Then the pain shows up in the body falling sick, a car crash happens and they are injured, or some other event. They 'hit the wall' and only then do they begin questioning everything they thought was so secure.

When the labels start showing themselves to be false, it's painful, yes. But if you understand what is happening, it's possible to recognize this 'pain' as a healing crisis. The 'split' mind is healing.

Q. *We can't do anything to speed up the falling away of these labels then?*

A. Understand first that the labels are unreal. Try and hold one of your identities, or put it in a box—you can't can you?

Q. *No.*

A. They're always changing, so they can't Be real. The misperception that you Are these labels happened despite you. So how do you think you can affect their falling away by anything 'you' do?

Imagine that I take you into a room in which there is a huge pile of eggs. Now I tell you that in one of these eggs, is the knowing of who you are. What will you do?

Q. *I'll break them all as fast as I can to find that one.*

A. Won't you perhaps put each broken egg aside and keep it, just in case you overlooked the one in which the knowing is? After all, you have no idea what this knowing might look like.

Q. *Yes, I suppose so.*

A. Now, what if I tell you that the moment you crack the egg that has the knowing in it, you will disappear. What will you do now?

Q. *I'll do it anyway.*

Q. *(another participant) I might have to think about that.*

A. You see, the pseudo-identity, who you think you are, obscures the Real you. If I told you that your eyes are the reason you can't see something, would you goudge them out?

Q. *No.*

A. This is because you are certain that seeing is only possible *because* of the eyes, isn't it?

Q. *Yes.*

A. What I am telling you is that who you think you are is not You. In order to know who you Really are 'you'—the false self—has to disappear. Can you cause this disappearance?

Q. *No, I can't.*

A. This is because you didn't cause yourself to appear in the first place. You also didn't cause the experience you have of yourself. You didn't cause all the thoughts you have about yourself to arise either, did you?

Q. *No, I didn't.*

A. So, you didn't cause yourself, and don't cause the thoughts you have about yourself.

Q. *No.*

A. How then can you cause anything to happen? How can the mind, which is not the cause of thoughts, cause them to disappear? How can you, who are not the cause of yourself, cause yourself to disappear? There is no way this can happen. This means that there is nothing to do, and nothing to avoid doing. As 'you' happened despite yourself, so actions happen despite you. Where is there any question of what action to take? You have no say in the matter, and you never have.

Q. *But that leaves us helpless.*

A.   Yes, you are both helpless and impotent. You have absolutely no control over anything. You ask, "What should I do?" only because you believe you have personal control. The first thing you can 'do,' is recognize that control is an illusion. This understanding may be grasped intellectually now, but it can't be *made* to go beyond understanding.

All you can 'do' is recognize the paradox of what you believe to be real. Relativity, or appearances, are only possible because of Reality. Reality is That in which appearances arise.

You've spent your life thinking 'you' are real. Mistaking an appearance for that which underlies it. This misperception happened despite you. But you could not even have this misperception if you did not experience 'I Am,' could you?

Q.   *No.*

A.   So begin there, with 'I Am.' Investigate how this experience of beingness came about. Your parents came together and chemicals mingled and a body appeared. In time this body will 'die,' but you will have no experience of the cessation of Being. You have never had an experience of not Being have you?

Q.   *No.*

A.   Therefore, how can you be sure that you did not exist prior to the body?

Q.   *I can't. But I only know experiencing through a body.*

A.   Until now you believed, with absolute conviction, that you were an object. Now you are beginning to realize that this is a misperception, aren't you? You've probably thought, "This is how it is," many times in your life, and then later on 'changed your mind.' Isn't that the case?

Q.   *Yes.*

A.   Then what is stopping you from at least considering that you might have existed before the body? You have nothing

135

to lose—except maybe your mind!

Q. *Yes, the mind feels so confused.*
A. The mind is confusion, as long as it is split, thinking you are an object capable of perceiving other objects. You can't stop struggling by struggling. You can't stop trying to control by using control. Similarly, you can't go beyond confusion by means of confusion. You can't understand your non-conceptual Self by means of the conceptualizing mind.

The good news is the mind is able to see the illogicality of itself when such investigation happens. This is all that is possible for you right now; to unravel the mind until it is seen to have no real substance.

Q. *Won't I feel like I'm going insane? What is sanity then?*
A. Sanity signifies the lack of mental extremes. The split mind can only think in terms of this concept versus that one. This means that the mind of anyone who is identified with the body is always thinking in extremes. The majority of people in the world must therefore be considered 'insane.'

Q. *That makes sense (laughing).*
A. When you unravel all the concepts that have arisen in the mind, you recognize the insanity of the mind. One could say that by means of this investigation, the mind is 'regaining sanity.' Do you see that here is yet another paradox? The mind is insane, an extremist, and might only be said to be sane when it recognizes its insanity!

We've thrown enough concepts into disarray to keep you busy for a while. Just don't think you have 'gained' any understanding in all this.

Perhaps recognize only, that you're more deeply aware that you understand nothing. Only in regression might the mind be said to be making any progress!

Awareness

It's a commonly held belief that awareness is some-thing that decreases and increases. This means that it is thought of as a commodity—something personal that can be manipulated and controlled.

When people own something they like to measure its value. Nowadays, because spirituality is considered the worthiest of goals, its value is also measured. This measurement is gauged in 'levels' of awareness.

Meditation, right eating and disciplined exercises seem to alter awareness. You focus within and awareness appears heightened. If the mind is distracted by external objects, awareness appears to decrease. As 'more awareness' is the goal, anything you do to serve this end is considered spiritual and important.

Now let's substitute the word awareness for experiencing. It may seem, when you are acting in certain ways, that experiencing is heightened or decreases. But if you think about it for a moment, you will realize experiences simply *change*. Experiencing doesn't stop and doesn't become something other than experiencing.

If you think about awareness in this way, you realize that all there is (while you have a body) is experiencing. All the varied experiences that happen are only possible because you experience being. This beingness is constant and unaffected by all the different experiences you have.

When waves appear on the surface of the ocean and then subside you might say that the ocean has changed in appearance. You certainly can't say that while there are waves the ocean is no longer an ocean. Similarly, experiences are only possible because you experience being—'I Am.' Like waves on an ocean, various experiences arise within the experience 'I Am.' When certain experiences stop, the experience 'I Am' is still there.

It's interesting isn't it, that so much attention is given to inconstant experiences and the need to control them. Meanwhile the experience of being, which is crucial to the perception of any experience, is ignored.

You think both 'you' and awareness are commodities. "I Am some-thing that is very aware." "You are some-one who is unaware." When you think you own something, it is human nature to want to control it. By attaching value to both commodities ('you' and awareness) you stay stuck in trying to manipulate both.

The paradox is, while you think of yourself as an object controlling awareness, you remain unaware of who you Really are. Awareness of self—'I Am'—ceases at the death of the body. You never have any idea of how long the body is going to last. This means that awareness is also something you never really have control over.

If something comes and goes you think of it as relative, but not real. If control is only partial can it be said to be real control? If experiencing of self ceases at the death of the body, can it be said to be real?

Here you are focusing on controlling two ever-changing objects. At any moment both could cease being experienced. Yet you cling to the idea that control is important and real. If you investigate control in this way, it becomes clear that you are fighting a battle with a foregone conclusion.

There has never been a time in your life where experiencing was absent. You have no sense of anything prior to experiencing. Apparently it began in-utero, but can you be sure of this? When your body emerged from your mother's body you had no sense of self as an object. Nor did you have any sense of separation from the mother. There was simply unlimited experiencing.

As you know from your own experience, nothing can be said to happen unless it's being perceived. A perceiving principle has to exist *before* any object is perceptible. Following this line of thought, it is simple deduction that a perceiving principle had to exist before the first awareness of 'I Am' was possible.

Until now, you may not have thought all this through, but perhaps you are beginning to see how ridiculous the idea is that you are an object. You cannot Be an ever-changing thing. You can't even be 'I Am,' because it ceases when the body dies. You can only Be the perceiving principle of all this.

The word Be means 'to exist.' It doesn't mean 'to come and go,' but signifies a constant. Right now the only constant you know is the experience 'I Am.' Within this experience arise various experiences. A movie that has constantly changing images is still a movie. Similarly, 'I Am' awareness, having various awarenesses, is still 'I Am.'

Do you see you have been focusing on what is changing about you, rather than looking at what is constant. If you want to know what is real you have to look for constants. While you are in a body, the constant and only experience that doesn't need validating is the experience 'I Am.' Strange, isn't it, that people spend so much time trying to control their varied experiences in order to validate their existence.

That the awareness 'I Am' one-day appeared, confined to an individual body, happened *despite* you. Where does the belief come from that says you can now control the way in which experiencing happens? Thoughts of control arose *despite* you, as do all beliefs. You are constantly thinking and yet the thought, "Where do thoughts come from" is a rare thought. Clearly, there is no answer to this question. Ah, and there you were thinking you had control. You don't even know where this thought came from! Ignorance is normally described in terms of 'lack of awareness,' but now perhaps you are beginning to see that even ignorance requires awareness.

How can you think of yourself as being more, or less, aware? You can only Be awareness, and however much experiences change, the *experiencing* of them is unaltered.

As long as you give value judgments to awareness you are focused on yourself as an object perceiving the commodity of awareness. While the body exists, all there is Is experiencing. Within this experiencing arise various experiences, but they are fleeting and so not Real.

The only constant experience you have right now is 'I Am.' Doesn't it make more sense to investigate this constant, rather than expending all your energies on inconstants? When 'I Am' awareness is no longer attributed with labels—'I Am this and that'—there is peace. You know this when you are on vacation and simply 'hanging out.' All thoughts of controlling leave you and you are happy to just Be.

The only reason you don't experience underlying peace all the time is because you are fixated on good versus bad experiences. If experiencing is all there is (while you are in a body) doesn't it make more sense to enjoy everything that arises in it?

If someone handed you a moon-beam would you stress yourself out trying to catch another better one? You already Are, in the awareness 'I Am,' and yet you spend all your time thinking about 'becoming more aware.' You don't want this experience because you prefer that one. All the time experiencing is happening, but it remains superficial. No-thing is experienced fully because you are so busy rejecting this experience and clinging to that. You don't ask "How is this experiencing possible at all?" This is because you KNOW that 'you,' the body object, is the cause of it! Do you see the ridiculousness of this?

It's believed that *the body* object (the 'me') will 'attain' a special state of awareness in enlightenment. So you meditate and eat right and do good acts and think this will set you up for your goal. The question is WHO is doing all this?

Your essential nature has to Be that which animates the body. If you were the body, you would have to describe yourself as a constantly changing *thing*. Which is, of course, what you do all the time. 'I Am depressed,' 'I Am fat,' 'I Am very spiritual.'

Be as you think you should be and the mind will remain focused toward objects and the need to control them. This describes involvement. BE as you Are, and there you are Being without any vested interest in controlling any-thing. This describes Presence.

To be void of involvement doesn't mean sitting back and allowing someone to beat your body to a pulp. This does not mean you won't bother eating or bathing. The natural preservation instincts and practical concerns of maintaining the body will not disappear. The taking of practical steps to nurture the body will continue as before. What will cease is the desire to avoid this feeling and maintain that one. Experiencing is rich in variety and when no feelings are held onto or rejected, there is no experience of limitation.

Be as you think you should be and you will remain feeling separate, limited, and struggling. Be as you Are, and there you Are 'open' to life as it presents itself. Then the concepts of freedom and limitation will have no meaning for you.

There is no 'experiencer' and no-one to be 'experienced.' Within experiencing, the *seeing* of individual objects happens. Within experiencing, the *hearing* of individual sounds, the tasting of different tastes, and the feeling of different sensations, arises. BE as you Are, and there you Are being, seeing, feeling, hearing, tasting, touching, acting, and thinking.

It may seem as if changes in your body and your objective world incur changes in 'you.' It only exists because you think 'you' are the body. As experiencing is your essential nature, this perception is a faulty one. If you freeze water it is still water. If you fashion gold into a bracelet, it is still gold. Likewise, even when feelings vary, there is still only Experiencing. Experiencing is all there Is as long as you have a body.

Like someone looking for their eyeglasses when they are on the end of their nose, you search for the Self. Your focus is split between the 'you' object searching and the object of your search. You blame circumstances, others, and yourself, when you don't find what you're looking for. In the meantime the fact that seeing is making this search possible is completely ignored. You don't question it or ask how it's happening. You are too intoxicated by the 'you' object and its quest.

Between seeker and Sought is Seeing. The 'seeker' is always changing. The 'Sought' is never found because the seeker's time is spent focusing on individual experiences. The seekers personal 'progress' is being compared to the 'progress' of others. Isn't it odd that the *impersonal* Self is what is sought, yet you think you can find It by means of adding to your *personal* accomplishments? Meanwhile, seeking is happening, but the question is rarely asked, 'how is the experiencing of this possible?'

Simply showing up for life is all that is necessary and it happens despite you, as it always has. Be as you Are, Experiencing, and the mystery of existence is solved. Focus on Be-coming, and you will continue questioning the meaning of life and your existence.

As a seeker you are like a detective seeking to solve a mystery, while ignoring the evidence that's right in front of him. The mystery is only evident because you Are. Yet you continue wondering 'who Am I?' wanting a conceptual description of the nonconceptual You.

Intuitively, you are on the right track if awareness is your focus. IF you're still thinking of awareness as a personal commodity to be increased, you are way off track. The good news is that this 'track' has no beginning or end and you Are the destination. The bad news for the ego, is that this can only be realized once you stop fixating on Be-coming 'more aware.' Instead you must begin asking, 'how is the awareness of Being possible?' 'To whom does this awareness occur?'

142

This article was written because of a request from John Veltheim for Esther to address the subject of 'Being Present' as a health care practitioner when 'treating' a patient. It was originally published for BodyTalk practitioners to use as a guide to understand the nature of what they are 'really' doing in treatment procedure. This will be seen to have application in all aspects of life.

Being Present

Each action precipitates a reaction and this process is called 'cause and effect,' or synchronicity. As long as the word *cause* is personalized, and synchronicity ignored, you believe you can, by your own volition or will, *make* things happen in life.

Whether Reiki, BodyTalk, or any other modality is used, specific actions appear to result in an effect on the patient. If a practitioner believes actions are effected by personal will and intent, she simultaneously believes that she is the cause of results that occur. When this is the case, the practitioner can only act from a place of involvement, and can never be said to be present.

There is a big difference between being involved and being present.

For example, if you have a small child who is having problems at school, there are various ways of addressing the situation. You can worry about him or you can admonish him.

"How can I help him feel better?"

"Why can't he be more like other children?"

"What have I done to cause this?"

"How can I 'fix' this problem?"

Either way you will appear to fuss over the child, and your interaction is one that is fuelled by the need to attain a specific result. As soon as need is combined with intent, focus is lost. This is because your mind is split between personal fears (overreactions) and personal expectations. This describes involvement,

143

and your over-reaction will probably be mirrored by your child.

An alternative way of dealing with a child's problem is to remain present to the situation, consulting the child as to his feelings. Then you may offer the child various options as to how to resolve the issue. The child may ask you to intervene, or may discover a way of dealing with things on his own. Either way, the interaction between parent and child has been exactly that—an interaction. Not two over-reactions. The child has participated in decision-making with the parent. Whatever the outcome, it is more likely to be one that occurs via mutual, focused, practical steps rather than involved over-reaction.

If, as a practitioner, you believe your role is to 'fix' your patients, this will be your intent. Which means you cannot be focused on the practitioner/patient interaction. You can only be 'focused' on what 'you' seem to be doing to the 'other' person and the results 'you' get.

If you close your eyes for a moment and focus on BEING, you will discover that the experience is not confined within your body and does not stop at the person next to you, or anywhere beyond your body. Every-one has the same experience when doing this exercise. This tells us that Consciousness is all there Is. It is only the idea that awareness is personal that causes the idea of limitation and the need to control.

As long as the practitioner believes "I Am causing" results, they are acting from the standpoint of personal limitation. You may feel you have the power to cause healing. If this is your belief, you cannot be free of the belief "What happens to the patient is 'my' responsibility."

When you personalize the 'treatment' process in this way, you are more likely to feel drained as the result of treating. When you personalize any action, it requires increased energy on your part because your personal identity is at stake. "I must do this," "I should have done that." Involvement (the need to control) is draining because it isn't natural. How can someone in such disharmony themselves ever hope to 'harmonize' any-one else?

Where BodyTalk is concerned, the innate wisdom directs all actions. The practitioner simply acts as a medium for these actions. In the case of Reiki, the energy goes to where it is needed, despite any intent you may have. When treating someone with Reiki, the practitioner also receives a 'spin off' of Reiki, and therefore a treatment. This makes these two highly effective modalities wonderful examples of the power of uninvolved interaction. IF this understanding is clear the practitioner recognizes that 'treating is happening,' rather than thinking, "I Am some-one treating some-body else."

Whatever your modality, if you have been practicing for a while, you will know that specific results are never guaranteed. This tells you that the precise effect of any action is un-assured. If you believe you can, and should, obtain specific results, your mind is forward focused. *Your mind is split between your identity (as a practitioner) and your personal goal for the patient. In other words, the process of 'treating' is far from focused.*

The desire to feel 'One' with the world and others is a sign that you intuit your sense of separateness to be unnatural. From a philosophical standpoint, the sense of separateness is a disease—a misperception. The instinct to feel at one with life, consciously or unconsciously, fuels all actions. You are constantly trying to bridge the perceived gap between the world and yourself.

As long as the mind is split between 'me' and 'others' you feel the need to control and modify your life experience.

The desire to heal the separation between self and 'others' is merely a reflection of the mind's 'split' between your true nature (the impersonal Self) and the person you think you should be (the personal self).

The belief that you need to become a certain way in relation to others keeps the mind distracted from who you Really are, beneath the personal facades. One of the mind's favorite distractions is to help others 'become' better or healthier.

Therapists and practitioners are engaged, perhaps more than most, in *apparently* 'healing others.' This is indicative of a very strong desire, albeit often unconscious, to heal self. The desire to harmonize external imbalances simply mirrors the dynamic of the 'me' identity, blindly seeking the impersonal Self and thus harmony.

When the Atman or Self is 'realized' it is clear that all happenings are spontaneous, synchronized and impersonal.

Manifestation (duality) does not disappear because of this 'realization.' The richness of duality continues unfolding within Consciousness. The difference is, that there is no desire to control *any* happening.

Practical steps are still taken, for example, to dress warmly when it is cold, to avoid having the body hit by an oncoming truck, but there are no *needs* with regard to obtaining specific outcome. There may still be a requirement to earn a living so that one can eat, but if money problems arise they are dealt with without fear—practically.

Experiencing continues, as before, with so-called 'good' and 'bad' experiences, but it is completely uninhibited by personal desires and fears. Everything happens as it happens and the body is the instrument through which situations are dealt with in a practical way, as they present themselves. This describes Being present.

The difference between the common man and the 'sage' is simply that the latter is uninvolved and totally present.

The common man is almost always involved, struggling between past feedback and yearned for goals. He lives with one foot in the past and one in the future—*filling the void.* What percentage of your thoughts are about 'what was,' 'what is not,' and 'what might be'? Your answer will give you a measure of your involvement. It will, of course, also show you to what degree you are present.

If you deeply understand that *essentially* there are NOT TWO —that there is no 'other,' only impersonal, unlimited Consciousness—then needs and intended outcome will dissipate.

This understanding is unlikely to happen until you put the physical body into perspective. To this end, let's say you make a robot. Before you wire it up and press the 'on' button, the robot doesn't and can't move. Obviously, this is because it's an inanimate object. Once electricity flows through it, it will be able to move in various ways—walk, pick things up, maybe even talk. Despite these actions, clearly, the robot doesn't feel anything. It's simply an inanimate object receiving animation from an external source.

Similarly, the body is an inanimate object that only functions when it is animated by Consciousness. In the same way your robot can't feel the electricity that courses through it, the body object feels absolutely nothing. Momentarily, your mind may rebel when you read this. But you know from personal experience that when a body is called 'dead' it's because Consciousness, or the sense 'I Am' has ceased happening in it.

Simple logic tells you that, if the body needs Consciousness to be animated, and is inanimate without it, it has ALWAYS been an essentially inanimate object. As a practitioner, if you understand this simple process of deduction, your way of treating will change. You'll stop focusing on making the body feel a certain way.

As a further illustration, you know that your television isn't the generator of the pictures that animate it. Your TV is the 'receiver' of the generator's signals. When you adjust the settings on your TV (such as color and hold) you focus on the clarity of the pictures. You don't expect changes to happen to the actual TV screen. You know the screen is just the medium upon which images appear.

Perhaps, as a practitioner, you have, until now, been involved in improving the physical body so that the 'person' will feel better. If this is the case, it means that you have been thinking of the body and its animation as one and the same thing. Or you could have been thinking the body was causing the animation.

These paradigms make about as much sense as someone who prods and pokes their TV screen in order to get a better picture. If you understand this, a paradigm shift will occur in the way in which 'treating' happens.

While you believe you Are the practitioner with personally directed skills, actions are involved—efforted. This dynamic is evidenced by the words so often used by practitioners—focus and intent. To use these two mutually contradicting terms in conjunction with one another makes no sense.

Focus means being present to what is Now. Intent signifies the mind's objective in the future. The use of these two words together is yet another indication that the mind is 'split.'

What has caused this 'split' is the belief that 'you' and 'others' Are objects with feelings. This has lead to the thinking that 'you,' the object, can control and alter what feelings take place in the 'other.' As long as the belief in personal control exists, you are never free of involvement.

If you deeply understand that *all* actions happen despite, albeit via, the body, focusing will gradually become the modus operandi. Rather than one object affecting another, there will be 'treating happening.' Minus personal involvement, the practitioner's body is a clearer medium for the impersonal functioning of Consciousness.

When a practitioner's personalized role is out of the picture, the patient is no longer treated as an object. When this happens, not only are 'you' focused, but your patient will probably experience feeling deeply focused too.

Relatively speaking, the body object *appears* affected by certain techniques. However, changes in the body are not felt in any way by 'it.' The body has simply become a more finely tuned vehicle for the impersonal functioning of Consciousness.

In BodyTalk, manifest-Consciousness is termed 'innate wisdom.' Via the body (by means of muscle testing), innate wisdom tells the practitioner what needs addressing. When rigid thinking is ready to fall away, 'innate wisdom' indicates this. Then a 'consciousness treatment' registers as a priority. When this happens, it means that the patient's body is *already* a clearer vehicle for the expression of Consciousness.

The 'treatment' protocol then serves to re-orient the mind within Consciousness. As 'mind' is merely a reflection within Consciousness, the change is only a relative one. Consciousness hasn't changed in any way, but the mind's interpretation of it has.

Consciousness doesn't need any-one to 'shift' it. There Is never any-one doing anything to an-other. There are merely actions happening within Consciousness that are not in any way separate to Consciousness. In the same way water cannot make itself more wet, Consciousness does not need to make itself 'more conscious.'

The intellect is the light of Consciousness, which reflects in the physical brain and body. When these two mechanisms are out of sync (not communicating in harmony) dis-ease results. BodyTalk *appears* to realign these mechanisms so that the light of Consciousness (intellect) manifests with greater clarity through them. When this happens, the patient feels 'more centered.' Then healthy body/mind communication results in healing. What is being healed is the 'split' mind, and its misinterpretation of Self.

This doesn't mean that you can 'cause' someone to Self-realize by treating them with BodyTalk—or any other modality. If the 'split' mind is healing, this occurrence is spontaneous. Whatever treatment process may have coincided with this happening has nothing to do with volitional acts.

The body is a phenomenal appearance within Consciousness. When changes appear to take place in a body after 'treating,' it is simply that Consciousness is animating the body in a different way. The coincidence of two unique expressions of Consciousness (practitioner and patient) is a spontaneous effect of Consciousness.

When treating is happening, Consciousness is both the effect and the affect. The physical body is the medium Consciousness uses to play within itself. Within this 'play' Consciousness identifies with the body and then dis-identifies from it. The 'me' identity has never been any Real happening. So, no individual 'me' can affect disidentification from the body or affect the body in any way.

As your role as practitioner continues to play itelf out, it is helpful to understand this paradigm. At first you may ask, "So what is the point of treating?" There is absolutely no point in treating, and no point in avoiding treating. The whole dynamic is just Consciousness at play.

If this helps you realize that no-thing is important, it doesn't mean you will give up doing anything. You have never had a choice as to what you do or don't do. All this realization may do is give you a better perspective on the 'importance' you may have been giving to 'fixing' the body. As this perspective increases in clarity, you will 'treat' from a place of impartiality—non-involvement. Then, anything can result and nothing may result, but you will not care either way. Paradoxically, this describes true caring—impartiality, neutrality and Being present.

Being in the Now

In my chapter *Being Present* I wrote of the difference between focusing and intending. The idea of focusing on what is, rather than what might be, is a helpful one to remember. As the practice of focusing dissolves the habit of intending, life is lived more fully, with less struggle.

If you try focusing you will find that focusing is not something that you can make happen. Focusing happens only when 'trying' is absent.

As the habit of intending is, for many, a long-standing one, it may not fall away easily. The frustration of this often serves to exacerbate the 'problem.'

I put the word problem between quotation marks to signify that problems are only a concept, a perception. The idea that anything is a problem arises within awareness, which is untroubled by any-thing. This article is to help you understand that any seeming , or difficulty, is merely a faulty perception—an illusion.

As an illustration, think of the ocean with its myriad colors. Some days you look at it and it is dark and stormy, full of grays and dark greens. Other days it is turquoise, blue, and pale green. These colors appear in the water, but if you try to isolate them, touch them, or extract them, you cannot. If you take a bowl and fill it with water from the ocean, the colors change. Maybe the color of the bowl is predominant in the water. Maybe you see your face reflected back at you.

Now ask yourself, "Has the water Really changed?" Clearly there is a relative change, but essentially the water is still water. There is a big difference between relative changes and Real changes. The word relative pertains to the objective, ever-changing world.

Real, with a capital 'R' pertains to the essential nature, which is unchanging.

When colors change in water, the water is still, essentially, water. Although colors appear in water they do not touch it and cannot be extricated. Similarly, awareness appears to happen 'in' the physical body. If you have never really thought deeply about what this means, you probably believe the body feels aware.

Awareness animates the body, much like the hand in a glove puppet animates the puppet. The puppet undergoes a relative change when the hand is placed in it and begins to move. This doesn't mean that any Real change has happened to the puppet. It is still essentially an inanimate piece of fabric, which appears animated.

The key word here is 'appears' which is very different to 'Is.' The body 'appears' animated, but it is essentially inanimate. Until you Know this you will continue believing circumstances can affect and even hurt you.

All you know with absolute certainty is 'I Am.' What you understand and believe right now is very different. You think, "I Am some-thing," which can be affected by the ever-changing world. You believe "When things are not going the way I want them to, life can affect and change Me."

The only truth you know about yourself is 'I Am.' This awareness is always there, whatever is going on in life. If you think of a time when problems appeared, you will realize that the awareness 'I Am' was essentially unchanged. You didn't stop feeling 'I Am' at any time. This means that no Real change occurred to You.

Relatively speaking, emotions may have spun out of control. Relatively speaking everything about your life may have changed. However the sense 'I Am' did not disappear.

'I Am' is what is essential about You. Without this awareness, there would be no perception of problems or anything else. In the same way colors appear in the ocean, but do not affect its essential nature, emotions that arise in the sense 'I Am' do not elicit any Real change.

If you struggle to 'be in the Now' it always appears that you are scattered—distracted by what was and what might be. Now recognize that this is simply an appearance in 'I Am.' When you add to 'I Am' the word 'scattered' it is because you are identified with the mind. This does not change the sense 'I Am' in any way.

When you focus on 'I Am' with your eyes closed, you discover that it has no location. 'I Am' may at first appear confined to the body, but if you sit for a while you realize it is not limited in any way. The sense 'I Am' is not isolated to the heart, does not stop at the skin, and doesn't stop anywhere beyond the body. Anyone doing this exercise makes the same discovery.

This tells you that 'I Am' cannot be scattered; that You cannot Be scattered. Scatteredness is simply a perception. The frustration of feeling scattered is simply a perception. When scatteredness happens, ask yourself, "Where is 'I Am' scattered to?"

Many years ago I wrote to my teacher in England saying, "I think I am going crazy." He wrote back, "Where would You go?" Clearly 'I Am' cannot 'go' anywhere because it has no location, no limitation. This being the case, how can You not Be in the Now?

The appearance of lack of focus is not a Real problem—it is a faulty perception. What is happening is that relatively speaking, you believe you need to Be a certain way. What you don't understand is that you are always Being. Just because the mind is turned toward the past or the future does not mean You are not in the Now. Where else could you possibly Be?

Clearly the need to focus would not present itself if you felt content and peaceful. You only think you need to do something if what Is doesn't feel comfortable.

Relatively speaking, there is a discomfort when the mind is struggling. Because you are identified with the mind you try to alter it. When you were born, and the mind wasn't full of beliefs, there was simply the sense 'I Am.' The mind's machinations are only apparent because of the sense 'I Am.'

As no words existed in the mind when you were born, 'I Am' was an awareness minus any words or concepts. 'I Am' happened before any concept arose.

When children first start talking they usually refer to themselves in the third person. That a child will say, "Mandy likes this," tells you they are not yet fully identified with the 'me' object. When awareness is conceptualized in 'I Am,' it is soon followed by, 'I Am this and that.' Before any concepts, 'I Am' was simply Awareness. Despite any concept, 'I Am' remains awareness.

If you want to give something an identity you have to talk of that which is constant about it. To believe you are a child today, then a teenager, and an adult after that, points to a relative (changing) identity. These labels you add to 'I Am' do not describe what is Real and unchanging.

What is constant about You is 'I Am' and this is your essential nature. Who you Really are cannot NOT be in the Now because by virtue of Being you Are here and Now.

Stop identifying with what you are not. Find out who you are not, by process of eliminating that which is inconstant. This investigation will always bring you back to 'I Am.' This essential principle, 'I Am,' remains whatever changes APPEAR to happen. Any and all appearances can only happen because of the sense 'I Am.'

Stop concerning yourself with the relative, changing world. Change will never stop as long as 'I Am' is there to perceive it. It seems that you can cause change to happen, but did you cause the mind to start thinking? Did you cause the sense 'I Am' to arise?

What must concern you is not "How can I change this or that?" What must concern you is why 'I Am' needs anything to be a certain way. As no relative change affects 'I Am,' why do you perceive any problem? Who you Are, essentially, is unaffected by any change. Until you know this, change will always present itself as a problem.

Until you know—beyond a shadow of a doubt—that You are not a thing subject to change, 'problems' will continue to arise. Like the colors in the ocean, change appears to affect emotions—which appear to affect You. When emotions arise, recognize that 'I Am' has not changed, has not disappeared.

All you know for sure is 'I Am.' Do not focus on what you might be, or how you might be. This makes no sense because 'I Am' simply Is—unlimited and unchanging. What appears within the awareness 'I Am' cannot touch it. What appears within the awareness 'I Am' cannot affect it in any way.

You may think you are not focused, but this is merely an appearance interpreted as 'I Am not present.' This interpretation happens because you know, 'I Am.' When the sense 'I Am not present' arises, ask the question, "Where is the sense, 'I Am?'" Of course, you will realize 'I Am' Is—present.

Discover who you are not and while the investigation unfolds remember 'I Am.' Gradually you will become clear that emotions, changes, and all concepts leave 'I Am' unaffected. You are always focused, even when it appears you are not. This is because focus means, Being present. Where else could you Be but in the Now?

Between understanding all this and Knowing it, there appears to be a struggle. Remember that the struggle is only apparent because of 'I Am.' You struggle to know the Self, not realizing that the struggle appears in the Self, in the sense 'I Am.' 'I Am' is in no way affected or changed by this seeming struggle.

There is only the Self, and everything else is just appearances within that Self. There is only Now, an eternal Moment, that bubbles up and subsides into itself. How can you categorize 'I Am' into sections of 'I Was' and 'I Will Be,' when the sense 'I Am' has never changed?

The only reason time seems real is because you have believed "I Am some-thing subject to change." Time simply refers to the relative changes that appear in 'I Am' awareness. The concept of time has absolutely no affect on 'I Am,' and so You can never not Be here Now.

When you think 'problems' are affecting you, recognize that the sense 'I Am' has not changed. Discriminate between the relative and the Real by investigating who you are not. "What is unchanging about myself?"

I am sure you understand that 'I Am' here Now. The reason this understanding doesn't stop you from worrying about the 'next' moment is because you think experiencing is personal—controllable. You believe all the labels you have added to 'I Am' describe You. You believe 'I Am some-thing' that can be affected by circumstance, and so it continues to appear as if 'problems' are Real. Illusory ideas about the 'next' moment persist as long as you are identified with the ever-changing body and mind, which was, and might be.

'I Am' always Is and only identification with the relative, changing world stops you from simply enjoying Being here Now.

Author's Note

Before going to print I asked my husband, John, if he would include one of his articles—the "The Stages of Enlightenment." Consequently, I wish to give him a little introduction here.

He is a published author (*Acupuncture* and *The BodyTalk System*); his professional qualifications would easily fill a book.

When we first met, almost eleven years ago, it was like the meeting of two immovable objects. We used to joke that it would have to be 'all or nothing' if we were to survive each other's stubbornness.

To our total surprise, our joking turned out to be somewhat of a self-fulfilling prophecy. About a year before I met with Ramesh, John met his teacher, Wendell Henkel, in London. It was at this time that the relative 'process of awakening' began.

So it is not from the standpoint of his professional qualifications that John writes. Instead, as a unique and often humorous expression of Consciousness, he writes from impersonal Knowing.

This article is in response to many requests for the apparent different 'stages of Enlightenment' to be explained. Many 'seekers' have seen that there is often a big difference between the concepts put forward by the many 'Gurus' who write and teach. This can be very confusing unless you are aware of some fundamental concepts around this misleading concept— Enlightenment and other terms such as Jnani, Satguru, Self Realization, etc.

This article is by no means definitive and only represents observations. It does not necessarily represent the personal experiences of Esther. Esther only writes and talks from her own unique experiences and does not really subscribe to expressing views on concepts, such as the ones put forward in this article. She did, however, ask me to include it in her book, as she felt it could provide useful insights to help clear up a few common misconceptions.

John Veltheim

The levels of Enlightenment
by John Veltheim

This is a particularly interesting subject when you consider that the title of this article is, in itself, a paradox. As there is no such a thing as Enlightenment, how can there be levels of Enlightenment?

What it comes down to is that we very often have to speak in relative concepts in order to be able to communicate ideas and concepts that are helpful to the relative understanding of life.

Generally speaking, a 'fully' enlightened person is free of all concepts of perception and limitation. He/she lives in a state of permanent absolute underlying peace and have no sense of personal identification. They see consciousness animating the bodymind object much the same as a hand will animate a glove. They recognize that undifferentiated awareness uses the appearance of objects such as the body to experience self awareness. This also means that they can recognize their bodymind complex and identify *with* it. They certainly do not identify *as* the body. This is a huge conceptual difference.

Further, the sage recognizes that the mind only identifies with relative concepts and calls them reality. Reality is defined as that which underlies relative concepts. Reality is that which is never changed by time. Concepts, such as the world we see, are in constant flux and change and, as such, are only relative concepts. Science clearly tells us that when we continue to break down matter, we reach the subatomic world in which there exists no-thing-ness. Simply, there is NOTHING there.

Once this disidentification with concepts occurs at the deepest level of *knowing*, there are many relative ramifications apparent to the sage and anyone who knows him.

The sage no longer identifies with concepts of right and wrong, freewill, guilt, freedom or limitation, and the absence of any other concepts.

Observation has shown that there seems to be a progressive falling away of the concepts which gradually leads to this eventual state of freedom from concepts, which is called enlightenment.

Just as each body and personality is unique, the process of 'enlightenment' is also unique to each person. However, schools of thought—such as the Vedantic school—have observed trends and characteristics that seem to follow some general patterns that can describe this unfolding process. These are the levels of enlightenment that will be discussed in this article.

It is very important that you understand that these are *descriptions* of what often happens. They are not *prescriptions* that will make it happen.

SETTING THE STAGE

We are all born enlightened and remain so throughout our life. Nobody *becomes* enlightened. All that happens is the covering of ignorance, caused by the faulty perception of concepts, falls away until we end up experiencing our natural state of being—so called enlightenment.

The baby is in the natural state. It experiences no limitations and just reacts naturally to life by experiencing joy, pain, and sensory input, without censorship or judgment. The baby is in the state I AM. Natural BEINGNESS.

In the first few years of life the baby looks out into the world, interacts with the people around it, and starts the first levels of identification: I AM—something. I am something different and separate from my mother: I am good, I am bad, I am in pain, I am this body, etc.

Judgment is eventually learned from the caregivers that assess behavior as good or bad, acceptable or unacceptable. We learn that some emotions please people, some make them displeased.

All these concepts and masks of behavior start to build up into a personal identity. This personal identification incorporates the body along with a set of concepts, belief systems, rules of behavior, anxieties, and attitudes; given to us by the people and culture that surrounds us through these formative years.

Concepts of self identification are reinforced when the people around us label us with those characteristics.

At this stage our essential nature has been clouded in this false identity—ME. The identity is false, because when we break it down there is nothing there but a bunch of concepts and labels. These constantly change throughout life. The concepts and beliefs held as a four year old are vastly different to the concepts of the teenager or adult.

It is strange that when people want to know their *real* self, they start looking at relative bunches of ever changing concepts. *Reality* is that which underlies relativity. Reality is unchanging.

We must ask ourselves: "What is the only unchanging reality of our life? What is the only phenomenon that has never changed since we were born?"

The answer can readily be experienced when we close our eyes and go introspective. It is our sense of BEING. Our I AM-ness. Everybody can always experience the sense that they exist. That inner sense never changes, and is there if we are happy, angry, sad, drunk…whatever. Further, it cannot be localized within any part of the body. It is limitless and experienced by everyone the same way. It is infinite REALITY!

Our dilemma is that because it is so apparently intangible, the mind cannot readily understand it. Our mind thinks in concepts and circles. It can't think infinity. It can't think absolute. It talks about the beginning of time and then wonders what happened an hour earlier. It thinks about the edge of an infinite universe and then wonders what lies a mile beyond it. It reads that there is no-thing in an atom and then calls matter *real*.

Because we identify with the mind, we try to use the mind to discover our true infinite nature. The mind simply cannot understand our true nature other than in concepts. Therefore the mind starts to look for concepts as an explanation. It starts to find labels, identities, rules, religions, and experiences that give the mind a feeling of importance and meaning. *It even believes that there must be a meaning to life.* This further builds up the false identity that further clouds our natural state.

In childhood we are trained (indoctrinated) in many of these concepts according to the prevailing conceptual trend of our community.

In early adulthood we may start to look elsewhere for other concepts, or may choose to simply indulge in our pursuit of the world of concepts. Simply live life in all its vicissitudes, emotions, and experiences.

In quieter moments we may feel lost, alone, empty, and without meaning. We sometimes get in touch with the underlying peace of the I AM, but interpret it as an empty void in an uncomfortable way. This can then lead us to filling in time with activity to 'fill the void.' Keeping the mind busy or even altering its state with drugs, chemicals, alcohol, compulsive behavior, and rigid dogmas, are simply tools to camouflage the big question—"Who am I?"

For most, this behavior continues in various forms according to culture and mental health until they die.

For some, the question "Who am I?" starts to nag at the deepest level – consciously or subconsciously. Experiences then start to happen. Shifts of consciousness occur. These can take many forms. They could include deep feelings of oneness with the universe when watching a sunset; religious experiences; drug experiences that are ecstatic; psychic experiences of apparent transcendence; or deep, non-mind insights into the nature of existence.

These peak experiences are often called 'shifts' of consciousness.

They then create a condition called 'seeking'. We are now miserable seekers!

The term miserable comes into the equation because the 'shifts' become the source of our next dilemma: The mind observes these shifts and enjoys them. It wants more. It tries to recreate them—often unsuccessfully, and so it then looks for more phenomena or techniques that will recreate them.

The mind will then pursue concepts to explain *it all*. It will look at orthodox religion, non religion, shamanism, Eastern religions, occult, metaphysics, new age techniques, meditation, and the list is as endless as the imagination of the mind.

The dilemma is that each of these concepts adds to the refrigerator full of concepts already in the mind. This increases the clutter that clouds us from our true nature. We talk of wanting to let go of the ME while we continue to strengthen the ME with more and more concepts. We increase our egotistical minds by giving it the satisfaction of being able to say such things as—"I can now meditate for two hours straight; I can sit in lotus position; I have atoned for all my sins by confessing to a God out there somewhere; I have traveled to eight different dimensions and talked to six angels, etc."

Each of these 'achievements' are fun, fill in time, create diversions, fill the void, massage the ego, entertain the mind, but, ultimately, take us further from our original goal: to answer the question "Who am I?' This is because these activities have added to concepts that distract us from our true nature that is always there, has never left us, is absolute reality, peaceful, and yet coated by the faulty perception of all these new concepts we have been chasing.

Fortunately, there is some good news.

THE FIRST STAGE OF ENLIGHTMENT: BUDDHI CONSCIOUSNESS

We must first realize that all this has been happening despite you. The concept of doership and freewill is just that—a concept. If there is nothing there, nothing is happening. If there is nothing there, nothing was born, nothing is really happening, and nothing dies—in REALITY

All happenings are appearances in relativity.

For some seekers, the first stage of enlightenment happens—despite their efforts—by Grace.

This stage usually has gradual onset and occurs in stages. The first stages are the peak experiences of life referred to earlier. These stages become more frequent and more powerful. They often involve feelings of deep bliss, peace, oneness, serenity, expansiveness, and similar phenomenal experiences.

At first these are short lived and can start early in life. Many children have these experiences.

Eventually they can start to be lasting and go on for hours, weeks, or months.

Usually, once they have become lasting, another phenomenon occurs: the deeper realization of the concept that you are the glove, not the hand that animates it. You are not the doer, you are being done.

This is the first deep non-intellectual realization that you are not actually in control of your life. That control is only a concept in appearance. This deep intuitive *knowing* brings great relief and surrender to life. It feels like the whole burden and stresses of life have been lifted from your shoulders. People entering this 'state' start using phrases like:

"I am not the doer, I am being done."

"It is not my will, it is the will of God."

"Thy will be done."

"Don't know, don't care."

"I have surrendered to God."

"I AM not this. I AM THAT"

The concept God can be substituted with other cultural concepts such as Allah, Source, Consciousness, Absolute, Ishwara, etc.

In most cases, there is a feeling of parallel worlds where there is a bodymind and, parallel to that, there is a higher force - a witness.

This person will often experience the concept of living in different dimensions. They become the objective, dispassionate observers of life—hence, the term—buddhi consciousness.

It must be emphasized here that, *at this level, the bodymind's collective concepts and cultural dogmas are still present.* (The AMness of habits are still there.)

Although there is a parallel world and the 'knowing' that all is not as it seems, they will often still interpret their experience in the language of their religion or cultural background and training.

Hence they could be a Catholic priest and interpret this as a state of divine grace (which it is) that has occurred as a result of their many years of prayer (which it probably has not).

He/she could be fundamentalist Christians who have experienced the concept of surrendering totally to God's will and are enjoying the unique phenomena of their religious (buddhi) state, because they no longer have the feelings of responsibility of being the doer.

If they had been studying eastern religions, they could easily label this as enlightenment although there will be some confusion because they will still be aware that they have concepts that are different to some of the Gurus they have studied. They may also be concerned that they don't necessarily fit in with the appropriate life style they have envisaged that an 'enlightened' person would live. They notice that they still have strong emotions and a desire to participate in the world like they used to. Although there are increasing periods of peace and bliss, there are also periods of mental turmoil and self-doubt.

The early buddhi state can be a mixed blessing. It can be the most exciting of all the stages because there is still bodymind concepts and emotional involvement stored in the body. It can also be frightening and confusing, especially if you do not have someone who has been there to guide and anchor you through this time.

The later buddhi stage is when the *knowing* of lack of doership and the impermanence of concepts becomes fairly permanent. Buddhi is never permanent and people can be in Buddhi for years and still come out of it. Some never get back into it. This is usually because the residual mental concepts took over and the mind won back its role as the foundations of the sense of—ME.

When in the buddhi state:

The person is often an excellent teacher and can often 'have' original thoughts and ideas.

Because the sense of personal involvement is so reduced, they tend to function better and go though life in a state of inspiration rather than perspiration.

They don't do things because they feel they should, they do it because they feel inspired to do it.

They tend to be more flexible about life, enjoy it much more in the now, and can experience intense peaks of bliss and other pleasant phenomenon.

165

They can also still be depressed, pessimistic, and have intense emotions.

It is also possible to be in the Buddhi state and not 'know' it. In this case the state is reflected in their casual, relaxed, uncontrolling style of life and in their tendency to spontaneity.

People in the Buddhi state can still have some very strong mental concepts about life and will often express those concepts convincingly because they are inspired by their *concept* of being directed by God, Source, etc.

They will claim that theirs is the ultimate state of enlightenment or realization and often then prescribe ways to help others 'achieve' this state. Usually this is based on their own personal earlier experiences. If they had a background of fasting, meditation, and running, then they will often encourage others to pursue the same 'pathway.' Others will have cultural backgrounds that make celibacy a necessity if you wanted to pursue your spiritual life because marriage and family would be a major handicap. Hence, in places like India, the tendency to see celibacy and vegetarian eating (because their religion forbids meat or vegetables are cheaper) as guidelines to enlightenment.

The buddhi state has the paradox of being a wonderful experience phenomenally—a true blessing; but, at the same time, since the relative process of self realization is incomplete, it can lead to many misinterpretations and misconceptions by well meaning people experiencing this wonderful state of consciousness. The Buddhi state can then become a source of frustration for the seeker who looks to these people for guidance.

Be wary of people who are too willing to give you prescriptions for enlightenment based on their experiences. Everyone is different—unique. You are already enlightened—you cannot attain it! The helpful sage is the one that focuses on destroying any concept you have. They may use concepts to do that, but will always warn you that any concept they use should also eventually be destroyed. When all concepts are gone, then the stage you are in is beyond the Buddhi state.

STAGE TWO: SELF REALIZATION

The Self referred to here is the Self with a capital 'S'. The self with a small 's' is the ego self of collective concepts. The concept we call ME.

The Self with a capital 'S' is the I AM. That which we experience briefly when we close our eyes and let go of conceptualization.

At this stage the 'witness' disappears. The concept of a God, Source, or higher power experienced in the Buddhi stage now becomes obsolete. The following dialogue arises in the mind:

Instead of "I am not the doer. I am being done." It becomes: "Who is not the doer of whom? Who is doing whom?"

Instead of "Thy will be done. And I have surrendered my will to God (Source etc.) The questions are, " Who's will?" "Who is there to have a will?" "Who is surrendering to whom?" "Why does there have to be will in the first place?"

Further, if God, Source, Consciousness, etc. is infinite, then how can I, or the bodymind, or any concept be separate from it? Infinity is just that—infinite—non divisible. Nothing can be separate from it; nothing can merge with it; no concepts have relevance to it. This means even the concepts of willpower, destiny, appearance, beginning and end, are all just concepts—not reality.

At his stage the Self is realized as indivisible. Concepts of separation from it cease and the Self Realized person only experiences the I AMness as a totality. All appearances in the form of different bodyminds are still perceived as unique expressions of awareness, but are not separate from the I AM.

However, in the first stages of Self Realization the AMness is still strong. This AMness relates to the concepts held in the bodymind as collective experiences and habits. They constitute the various involvements with emotions that have been stored. They include the unique concepts still being held around religion, culture, belief systems, and prejudices.

The I of I AM is the perception, and the AM of I AM is the AMness still being perceived.

At this stage there is a natural process of dissolution of the AMness. It first starts with the deep realizations that I AM *not* this or that. I AM *not* the body, the emotions, the beliefs, the religion, the concepts, the techniques, etc.

This starts the dissolution as a series of 'ah ha' paradigm shifts.

Further shifts happen when experiential phenomena occur such as bliss, and intense gratitude. Suddenly there is the realization that for bliss to be there, someone (a ME concept) has to be there to experience it. The bliss state then points out that we are not *there* yet because there is still a faint ME present. For gratitude, there has to be someone (a ME) experiencing the gratitude and someone (a separate *concept* such as a limited thing called God) to direct the gratitude toward. Again, this evidence that you are not *there* yet and that the mind is still playing its conceptual tricks. These intense peak experiences that seemed to draw you to this 'state', have now to be discarded also as they were only conceptual experiences of the mind's interpretation of enlightenment.

All this breaking down of concepts will now precipitate the spontaneous progressive dissolution of the AM factor in the I AM equation.

This will often rekindle an old friend that has probably been experienced before in the seeking stage: the Kundalini energy. This article won't discuss this big subject but, in simple terms. the Kundalini is intense energy that flows up the spine and chakras under certain circumstances. It has several functions.

This time its function is to burn out the tapes of AMness. This can be a very powerful and even frightening experience involving strong phenomenal changes to the body. Intense shaking, feelings like the head is going to explode, headaches, nausea, vertigo, diarrhea, and many other symptoms can be experienced. The worst part is that they do not respond to treatment because they are not a disease state.

The fascia of our body is really neuropeptide brain tissue and is where the bodymind has stored all these memories, experiences, and beliefs that we have become involved with in our lifetime. The mind has stored these to reinforce its sense of ME. This Kundalini experience can be very strong and can come and go for months or years during this phase. The length of time it takes and how it manifests is too big a subject for this article.

In a shortened version, when the AMness is burned out through paradigm shifts, Kundalini—or any other experiences—then all that is left is the basic AMness we were born with: our basic nature. This is going to be free of all the 'mind stuff,' concepts, and habits, we collected during our life. This is the stage of full Self Realization covered in stage three.

My own experience is that the density of the body seems to change. Years ago I experienced the phenomena of 'astral traveling.' During this experience you have the feeling of leaving the coarser body and floating. At some stage you have to return to the body, and the feeling is not very pleasant. You are going from a feeling of freedom and 'lightness' back into what feels like cold, dense, clay. This 'clay' is the collective emotions, experiences, and holding of the body. After some AMness has fallen away, the body feels lighter and less dense. You just keep feeling lighter and freer.

What you must be reminded of is that while all these relative phenomenon are occurring, nothing *real* is happening. Only relative concepts are falling away. The true *reality* is unchanged and unaffected. It was there when you were born, has never left you, and will be there—unchanged—when all the AMness of concepts have dissolved.

During the I AM phase certain relative phenomena usually happen. These can include:

1. The Bliss and other experiences diminish and the true I AM experience of total and absolute emptiness becomes the underlying 'presence' of the wakened state. This 'emptiness' is the *peace beyond understanding* because it is totally free of any experience. Therefore, it is absolute peace in a form that cannot be described with words.

2. The relativity of time is truly appreciated. The Self Realized person tends to experience, at the deepest level, that there is only *now*. Everything is experienced only in the now. Past thoughts and experiences are simply like distant memories that happened to 'someone else' and do not affect the now. Hence there are no experiences of guilt, anxiety, or involved emotions from the past. In the same

way, it is impossible to get *involved* with anything in the future. There can be planning and practical steps taken. What is impossible to create is a mental scenario of some dreadful happening to, say, a loved one or your business, and to then get emotional or upset about it.

3. As everything is experienced in the now, the emotions that are experienced are those that are related to something actually happening at that time. Further, there is no concept of ME to get involved with the emotion. The emotion just arises, takes its course, and falls. It is not stored, and never becomes a potential stress or pathology. Emotions are experienced without the censorship of the mind trying to alter them. As such, they are experienced fully and therefore the underlying experience is that of absolute peace. Even anger and grief are experienced fully with an all-permeating experience of peace.

4. As the emotions (AMness) disappear in the bodymind, they will no longer be there to resonate with the experiences of others. Therefore the sensation of experiencing the world and other people as emotions, tensions, etc., falls away. Psychic phenomenon and experiences disappear so that nothing disturbs the experience of BEING.

5. The thinking of the mind experiences a new phenomenon. It cannot maintain involvement in any unnecessary thought process. As soon as involved thinking starts, it is simply cut off. It can be likened to channel surfing the TV. You can never stay on one station. The mind just flits from one thing to the next. In this way the mind is childlike and the tension of involvement ceases.

6. There is no sense of freedom because there is no concept of limitation. The I AM is not limited in any way.

7. There is no concept of a personal God, Source, Universal energy, Light Being, or anything else. All of these concepts are nouns and, therefore, denote *things*. Things are finite and limited. I AM is infinite. You cannot speak of the omminescence of God and, at the same time, limit it to

being a thing.

8. Judgment falls away. As everything is now seen clearly as mere appearances in totality, there is nothing there to judge and no one to judge it. This means that everything is experienced as a simple spontaneous appearance in totality. Not good, not bad, not right, not wrong—and nothing to be changed.

9. Acceptance of what is, as is, becomes that natural state. There is no desire to change anything, and there is the realization at the deepest level that nothing can be changed in any way.

10. The mind can still be active and can still be quite a nuisance. Mental distraction and over-activity can still occur but there is no one there to worry about it, so that the intensity is not there. Nor is the desire to stop the activity of the mind. Thoughts are seen as the tension within the body and they tend to diminish as the AMness is dissolved. However, some thoughts will always be present for as long as there is a body. The body appearance is, in itself, a tension that requires thought forms.

At some stage during this I AM process, the mind ceases to question its existence. It realizes that it is only a function of the body. It is not you. The mind collapses with regards its aspirations of self existence and self importance. *This is a major turning point and it is the point where this process becomes irreversible.* (Up until that point, the process could reverse and the ME of the mind take charge again and the awakened state goes back to sleep.) When the ME of the mind has totally collasped, the next 'stage' has been reached.

STAGE THREE: THE JNANI

This is the level of full Self Realization, and in some schools of philosophy it is considered the only true level of enlightenment. Esther and I tend to agree that this is 'technically' the first stage of Enlightenment. The previous stages are reversible and there is still 'amness' present to experience the relative phenomena.

It is irreversible, total, and all questions have ceased. The AMness has now fallen away to the point that the Jnani is now the 'I'—the perceiver of the 'AM' plus enough AMness to contain their basic personality and the genetic traits they were born with.

At this stage the term Jnani is used. It means – 'one who knows'

The irony is that most people think that means they know a great deal or everything. What it really means is that they now 'know', at the deepest level, that they 'know' nothing. There may be much intellectual knowledge and understandings, but essentially they know that the true nature of life and existence cannot be understood with the mind.

Other than that, the relative process of this stage is just that the second stage—Self Realization, is 'completed.' The relative experiences are the same as the second stage.

[A little side note here to discuss the term Guru. This is often used in India, and can be confusing to the Westerner. Guru essentially means the 'dispeller of ignorance' or, in Western terms, a teacher. (We assume our teachers dispel the ignorance of our children!) This term is often used with the word disciple which, in the West, would mean student. Although it would be more correct to say that disciple, the way it is used with the term Guru, really infers 'devoted' student. The Guru to whom you are attracted can be at any of the stages described in this article. They can also be anyone, or any concept, that dispelled some ignorance throughout your life path. There is also the concept of the 'inner Guru', which relates to self learning and self awareness.

Further to this is the question—"Do we need a Guru for enlightenment to happen?" In traditional Vedanta philosophy there is a concept that you will never be graced by 'enlightenment' unless you have experienced the Guru. In this case, someone who is Self Realized or higher. This, however, apparently does not need to be a conscious meeting or experience. You may just happen to be on the same plane as a Jnani, and the experiencing will happen that 'kick starts' the process. I stress, however, that many very well informed sages have disputed that theory and consider the 'inner Guru' enough.]

STAGE FOUR: SAT-GURU

It is generally considered that when the Jnani stage is reached, that person will, at some stage, automatically enter the beginning of the Sat-guru stage. Most Jnanis seem to go into full Sat-guru months or weeks before they die. It is often seen by their students as a sudden change in their teaching style and disposition.

Some Jnanis have become full Sat-guru and stayed alive for many years. They have tended to be unknown, and do not generally appear in public, become famous, or live in ashrams. If they were a famous Jnani or guru, this is the stage they tend to become recluses.

The explanation of Sat-guru is difficult even for a Satguru, let alone someone like me who has not experienced it. Here are my thoughts on it from the observations and experiences with someone going through the Sat-guru level.

My 'understanding' is that the full Sat-guru often serves as the teacher of those people who are already in one of the earlier stages. Their teaching gradually becomes uncompromising. They accept no concepts, and even challenge the concept that there are concepts.

Their 'goal' is the elimination of all concepts. At the deepest level, they are aware that manifestation is appearance of nothing, out of no-thing-ness, and its return to no-thing-ness. In essence, nothing has been created, nothing has been born, and nothing dies. So what is all the fuss about?

In the full Sat-guru, all AMness has disappeared except that miniscule energy necessary for the bodymind to remain in appearance. Essentially, when they are on their own, they are like the perfectly calm pond in absolute peace. No thoughts, as we would recognize them. When somebody appears before them, a ripple is created on the pond to give them sufficient appearance of personality to interact. Once the interaction is completed, they return to silence. We are not capable of understanding what that really means, or feels like.

The 'I' of the 'I AM' in the Jnani now disappears as well. Remember that the 'I' was the perceiver of the 'AM'. In the Satguru, there is no concept of a perceiver in the first stages of Sat-guru. There is only 'perceiving' happening. At full Sat-guru even the 'perceiving' ceases. Now there is only 'IS'. This is beyond conceptualization with the mind.

Further, as their 'natural' personality disappears, the personality of those around them seems to disappear. They perceive less and less distinctions of individual personalities. Eventually, they literally disappear as a personality to others, and the other personalities effectively disappear to them.

All goals, desires, and concepts have fallen away. Dis-passion (impartiality) deepens.

The Sat-guru is only interested in dispelling concepts. The Jnani will often enjoy the dialectics of debating concepts and techniques, and tends to pursue ideas to create temporary understandings for the student. From this we have received some of the great teachings of some of the great sages of history.

The Sat-guru will not let the student stray far in concepts, and will continue to challenge the basic concepts, and even challenge why the question was asked in the first place. They see that understanding is essentially impossible and, therefore, the well articulated answer to a question ultimately only increases the covering of ignorance. The Sat-guru is happy to see the student totally confused and frustrated, and will not relent until the student's mind has totally collapsed. They know that only when the mind gives up all concepts, will there be peace.

Often times the Sat-guru prefers to teach in silence and just allow 'presence' to be imparted to activate the 'inner guru'.

They have no interest in concepts of stages such as those expressed in this article, as they are just more fodder for the mind. In the same way they do not involve themselves in pathways, techniques, religions, or any other conceptual pursuits.

There traditionally appears to be three or four Sat-gurus alive at any stage in history, and they appear to be part of the balance of appearance in manifestation.

SUMMARY

Buddhi (Enlightenment): I AM THAT
Self Realization: I AM
Jnani: I
Sat-guru: no conceptualization

CONCLUSION

This article is simply an exercise in concepts. It was designed to help dispel some other concepts you may have held, and perhaps provide you with some new ones to drive your mind crazy. It may have also held up a few useful signposts to help give perspective.

What must be remembered is that none of these concepts are the truth. Once something is expressed, its opposite is also true. Ultimately these articles, and attending Satsang, may serve to help destroy some of the concepts that you have which are limiting your expression of life. Eventually this may help you to realize, if only intellectually, that you cannot mentally understand life, or even who you are. That may then enable you to simply start living life, as that is all you really can do.

Illusion, relativity, and enlightenment

(and other misconceptions)

Many spiritual teachings talk of manifestation as 'illusion.' You probably interpreted this to mean that the world, as you know it, is unreal. This leads you to wonder what on earth the sage experiences when *he* 'realizes the world to be an illusion.'

If you show fifty people a Rorschach blot they will probably all see different images in it. This tells you that no-one sees anything in exactly the same way. But even this understanding doesn't help you grasp the idea that what you see as real, the sage sees as unreal. The only possible conclusion you can come to is that 'the sage is in an altered state.'

This is the huge misconception people have of enlightenment. When the sage realizes manifestation to be an illusion 'he' actually recognizes that his perception up until that point *was* an altered state. You see *the word illusion actually means 'faulty perception.'*

The realization that happens through the body of the sage, that 'he' is not any 'thing,' but Is *impersonal* awareness, expressing itself through a particular body. The sage isn't in any kind of 'state.' Only an object can be said to be 'in a state.'

The words reality and relativity now need to be looked at more closely. *The word reality means 'that which underlies appearances.'*

The word relative means something considered or having relation in significance to something else. To use the word relativity with regard to the manifestation is to denote the relationship of one thing to another. Another way of putting this is that manifestation is a relationship of appearances. Ah, and here you have been, all your life, thinking that appearances *are* reality!

The Knowing that the sage embodies is that Reality is NOT relativity. Manifest appearances are NOT that which underlies appearances.

This new understanding may not change your experience of manifestation. However it may cause a radical reassessment of the way in which you've thought about yourself and the world until now.

You think of yourself as a body-object, and an object is an appearance. If reality means that which underlies appearances, this means that who you think you are is unreal.

'You' are *relatively* real, but relative is the operative word here. The word relative means 'considered or having significance in relation to something else.' 'You'—the bodymind-identity is *relative* (an appearance) *in relation to* Reality (that which underlies appearances).

Right now you think of yourself as the body-object—an appearance. Until now you have thought of yourself as real. You have thought of relativity as reality. In other words – as ridiculous as they will sound—you have been thinking 'I Am an appearance' which Is 'that which underlies appearances.' Sounds ridiculous doesn't it?

You may not consciously have thought of yourself as being the body. Yet this belief is clearly evidenced by the way in which you fixate on changing and trying to control it. If you ask someone, "Who are you?" they usually tell you their name and point toward their chest.

Interestingly, no-one ever points to their head when they indicate themselves. Everyone, whatever their culture, points to the heart. Despite this universal instinct, most everyone is identified with the mind.

If you think of yourself as 'a caring person,' it may seem to you that you are identified with your heart. This is another misperception.

As my friend Vidya so beautifully puts it, "Thoughts are the sisters of emotions." You think, 'I Am caring,' but the 'caring' you are talking about is full of concern and worry.

You express 'caring' for someone by trying to *make them feel* good. You express 'caring' for someone by acting in particular ways. This is because your mind, not your heart, dictates that 'this is how it should be.'

The word should means 'duty or obligation.' Obligation means 'constraining power,' or 'burdensome task.'

Any time you use the little word 'should', you are inferring that 'an obligation is necessary.' Every time you use the little word 'should' you are inferring that constraint and burden is necessary. This means that day in, and day out, you are using a word that is strongly linked to the concept of guilt. This is because guilt means responsibility or obligation.

Bet you had never thought of it in this way before!

Now let's go back to the concept of 'caring' and link all this together. You think 'people should be caring.' This means that they have an obligation, a responsibility, to be a certain way.

As an example, let's say you are a vegetarian and walk through a meat market. Your thoughts may be "How cruel and terrible these murderers are." The thoughts of the butchers may be, "We're doing a good job putting food on people's tables." Who is to say which one of you is more caring?

The 'caring' that is happening in both parties is nothing more than a set of judgments. These don't come from the heart, but from the mind. If you think you are 'caring' by saving animals from being butchered, it may seem to make your heart feel better when you boycott a meat market.

All that is making your heart feel good is that you are feeling better about yourself. You KNOW you are not 'guilty' of doing such heinous acts. You KNOW that butchers are the guilty ones! This puts caring into a whole new light doesn't it.

How can you say this is real caring or has anything to do with the heart or with love? All this kind of caring is is self-serving judgments that decrease your own sense of personal culpability. 'I know *I'm* doing the right thing!'

I have avoided the use of 'God' as much as possible, simply because it is full of connotations of a personalized entity separate to you. Regardless of your present day beliefs, IF God was a part of your upbringing, it is helpful to put biblical terms into perspective.

Have you ever wondered what is meant by 'God is Love'? Because you think of love as the opposite of hate, the only way this statement can be understood is by interpreting it to mean that 'God is forgiving.' And this, after all, is the interpretation religions give to these words. That is, God loves 'you' enough that He can disregard 'your' sins.

Another statement in the Bible is that "God is omnipresent." This means that God is everywhere.

Now if God is everywhere, how do you think He perceives any-thing separate to Himself? As nothing is separate to Omnipresence, who is guilty and who is there to forgive?

*When it is said that "God Is Love," the word 'love' signifies
neutrality. It has nothing to do with the opposite of hate.
God is just another word for neutrality and neutrality denotes
'not helping or supporting either of two opposing sides.'
'God' recognizes no 'other'—only 'you' continue to
think in terms of 'me,' God and 'others.'*

Can you imagine being totally neutral? What would it be like to be amongst starving children in Ethiopia and be totally neutral and impartial? Do you think it means your heart would not feel and that you would sit there eating McDonald's and not giving a damn? Or would it mean that your mind would be void of judgment, and that actions could happen spontaneously—without you fussing and getting upset?

Just think about this. If someone is in distress, just because you experience neutrality—have no judgments—are you going to avoid helping them? Avoidance only happens when the mind judges that something *needs* avoided. Fussing and clinging only happen when the mind judges that something *needs* maintaining.

Love and caring, as you know them, have everything to do with the mind's judgments, neediness and fear of lack of control.

The sage is free of all judgments because 'he' Knows that there is no 'other' separate to 'him.' Knowing 'himself' to be no 'thing' and, therefore, unlimited, the sage embodies Neutrality. The sage Is the embodiment of the impersonal Love talked of in the Bible, and so misunderstood.

This is why actions that happen via the sage's body never have malicious intent, or any intent at all. All actions happen spontaneously – unimpeded by censorship and judgment.

The sage may appear to help 'others,' but it is never because the idea 'I should' has entered his mind. His mind is no longer split between 'me' and 'others' and so the concept of guilt is totally foreign to him. This is why there is no perceived need to judge any action that happens through his body, in-relation-to another body.

As long as you link the word 'should' to caring and loving, you will remain blind to Your neutral, impartial Self. It's said that 'love is blind,' but has the way in which you love ever remained 'blind' to judgment and need for very long?

While you are identified with the sense of a 'me' separate to 'others,' you can never experience neutrality and impartiality. While the mind is 'split' you can never experience love without need.

Life, as you know it, is being lived superficially at best. You are identified with superficiality—appearances. In order to know who you Really are—underlying this appearance—you have to look at what is constant about you.

The only constant you know, that no-one has ever had to prove to you, or teach you, is the knowing 'I Am.'

The sense 'I Am' is the only constant, unchanging experience you have ever known. Just because you have added labels to it ('I Am in pain,' 'I Am lonely') you think the experience of Being changes. All that has been changing are the labels you have added. In order to experience these labels your sense of beingness is necessary.

How you perceive your sense of beingness is similar to the way you might look at the sky from your back-garden. From your limited perspective it appears as if the sky stops at the earth. From the limited perspective of thinking you *are* the body, you

181

can only conceive of 'I Am' awareness as being contained by, and limited to this body.

If you were in a space ship your whole perspective on the sky would change. You would see that all the planets and stars are contained *within* the sky. It would be clear to you that the sky is in no way limited by any objects appearing in it.

Via the body of the sage, the 'big picture' is evident. The body is no longer seen to contain and limit awareness. Rather, there is the Seeing that the body and all objects are appearances *within* awareness.

The sense 'I Am' is the label given to awareness happening through your body. Without awareness, neither the body nor the sense 'I Am' would not be known. This means that awareness is both the effect (cause) and the affect (result) of these two perceptions.

> *Awareness is not-two and so cannot be altered and is not limited.*

To believe you Are the body object *causing* actions is to believe that an effect (appearance) can cause an effect (another appearance). Clearly, no appearance can cause another appearance.

Are you beginning to see how the misunderstanding of simple little words has kept you, your whole life, thinking in such back-to-front terms.

You are also identified with 'your' (personal) actions and roles. If this weren't the case you wouldn't feel guilty when actions are deemed deficient, or feel pride when actions are praised.

Actions define 'you' in exactly the same way the body defines 'you.' You take pride in the body when it is fit, muscular and slender. You feel guilty when you over-eat and don't exercise because you compare yourself to those with better bodies, who are more disciplined.

How can you possibly Be both an object *and* actions?

This isn't the sum of your misperceptions, because you also think you Are what you think. This is evident when you proudly say, 'I Am intelligent.' This is evident when you guiltily admonish yourself saying, 'I Am stupid and I know I *should* be able to figure this out.'

How can you possibly be an object *and* thoughts *and* actions? You can only Be the perceiving principle of all this.

You are identified with results—the body that resulted from intercourse, thoughts that resulted from studying, work that resulted from actions, body image that resulted from exercise. You focus on these results and judge them. Then you want to *cause* the results that define 'you' to be even better. Or perhaps you are so self-satisfied you just want to cling on and maintain the results 'you' have achieved. Either way, you are never free of judgment and the need to control.

By now you may be thinking 'I've got the point.' IF this were the case you wouldn't be commenting at all, because laughter would be all that was possible for quite some time.

If you intellectually understand you are not the body, and that you are non-conceptual, (not a 'thing') you may sum your understanding up in, 'I Am nothing.' This may be a horrifying thought to you, unless you recognize that, as a non-concept, You can only Be the impersonal (non-conceptual) awareness in which all concepts appear.

As this definition is merely a bunch of concepts it only points to the Truth beyond concepts. This means that none of these words can make the conceptual 'you' have the experience of the non-conceptual Self. All these words can do is point you away from what you thought you were. This is a start.

The more deeply you 'understand' who you are not, the stronger the desire becomes to know who you Really are. If you understand that your essential nature is uncensored spontaneity, you will perhaps realize 'you' can do nothing to *cause* or *control* realization of the Self.

Fortunately, the Self you seek is who You already are. You just don't know this because most of the time the you-of-false-facades obscures this fact. I say 'most of the time,' because you have frequent glimpses of your essential nature. This happens everytime 'you' lose yourself in an activity. At such times there is only awareness of the activity because you have forgotten yourself in relation to what is happening.

When someone calls your name, you remember yourself. Retrospectively you realize that actions were happening despite any conscious effort. Time seems to have flown, and even though it seemed just seconds it can often be hours that have passed.

Invariably, the minute you remember yourself you make a mistake and actions become efforted. In retrospect, you see that actions happened with more efficiency and no stress. When the personalized 'you' object is forgotten, actions continued happening via your body. Because the personalized 'you' object was out of the picture these actions must be called impersonal.

In your every day life, each time you forget yourself, you have retrospective glimpses of impersonal actions. They are stress-free, efficient and spontaneous. This means that you have endless glimpses of your essential, peaceful nature. Isn't it strange, that you spend so much time suffering, because you think personal control is vital to your existence.

A while ago someone wrote to me saying, "I don't think I would know my essential nature if it hit me over the head." What she was meaning is that the false personality was so habitual, she didn't know what personality characteristics were innate, or natural.

It isn't necessary to discover specific, innate personality traits. You simply need to recognize the times when self-expression is unaccompanied by thoughts of "Perhaps I should have said that," or "I should do this differently." At such times self-expression is spontaneous, stress-free and underlain by peace. Then all you have to do is watch when and why you censor those actions at other times.

Each time you recognize the censoring 'you,' censorship diminishes. No false façade can stand up to the light of scrutiny for long. That is, of course, unless 'you' start admonishing yourself for it, or thinking 'I *should* be making more progress.'

The idea of progress and shoulds and should nots have perpetuated this whole mess until now. If you start 'shoulding' on yourself, perhaps you will remember these words.

When the seeker learns he is not the body, or any object, he thinks, "Now I have understood something." And that is all that has happened. A new understanding has replaced the previous one. The seeker has not found what he is looking for, but for a while is content to take pride in 'having made progress.'

Ramana Maharshi used the example of digging a thorn from his foot with another thorn, to describe the process of weeding out false concepts. The trouble is, when your mind latches onto any new concept it gets excited. 'Now I know something important.' As soon as importance is given to any 'understanding,' it is similar to digging a thorn out of your foot with another thorn and then continuing to dig around in the wound with the second thorn.

If you understand that you are not the body and that actions happen despite you, don't cling onto this understanding. A seed has been sown in the mind that has dispelled a misperception.

A while ago someone told me, 'I know the 'me' will eventually disappear, but I just can't stop wanting it to happen faster.' Just know that the 'me' is simply a description of the body's relationship to other objects and concepts. You are always reassessing the 'me' and so it is always changing. This tells you that the me isn't anything Real. The 'me' doesn't underlie appearances; it *is* an appearance.

Don't fixate on the idea that the 'me' must fall away before you can Know who you are. Rather understand that it is unreal – an appearance only. Then ask, "Who is having this understanding?' This changes your entire focus, because you are not trying to rid yourself of some-thing that isn't there.

According first to philosophers and now physicists, the body, like any other object, is essentially empty space. If you break the compounds of the body down, only empty space is found. Relatively speaking, space is required in which the body can appear.

When the body dies, relatively speaking, some-thing has disappeared. In Reality, there has only ever been empty space or no-thingness. As the body itself is actually empty space, no-thing has been created, and no-thing has disappeared or ended.

When the 'me' identity is exposed as false, your natural personality traits, are expressed—minus censorship. Gradually this expression of individuality also dissolves. This dissolution happens spontaneously with the deepening of dispassion, or impartiality.

As individuality dissipates, gradually phenomenal experiences appear as little more than ripples on a pond. Experiencing and actions still continue, but all is witnessed from a virtually still point. All physical efforts arise from effortlessness.

The whole process from identification with the body to the realization that You are not 'it' may be likened to living on the circumference of a wheel and gradually moving toward its hub.

Without the hub of a wheel, its radius would have no support and could not exist. The hub of a wheel and its elements were first in-potential in the space that contains them.

Similarly, your body was first in-potential in Consciousness which was unaware of its Self. The sense 'I Am' happened when Potentiality activated in Self-consciousness via the body. Out of no-thingness the body appeared and is called some-thing. Self-consciousness then identified with this 'thing' and called it 'me.'

You know 'I Am,' but before this occurrence there was no self-consciousness. Self-consciousness is happening because there is a body through which awareness expresses its-self. How can you Be the body, or any-thing that is dependant on no-thingness for its existence? You can only Be that no-thingness, or Potentiality.

When this is realized there can be no question of a creator and creation, or birth and death. There is no intelligence deliberately activating Consciousness-unaware-of-itself into Self-consciousness. Spontaneity is perhaps the only word that can describe the activation of Potentiality into phenomenal manifestation.

The Knowing of your true nature is already there, but like some deeply buried treasure, you need first to uncover it. Your beliefs and accumulation of knowledge obscure the treasure of who You are. The question to ask is, who is experiencing this delusion?

Delusion signifies 'mental disorder,' and is a description of the split mind, torn between believing in a 'me' separate to 'others.' The mind of the sage is no longer split in this way.

When the 'me' is realized as false, the experience of having a personal body, unique to other bodies, doesn't stop. All that happens is the Knowing that relativity is NOT Reality.

Relatively speaking, a lot has changed because censorship is absent from the mind's thinking processes. *Relatively speaking,* a lot has changed because you no longer experience being an object desiring control. All desires have gone. *Relatively speaking,* tremendous tension will have left your body because you are no longer efforting to Be different to how you Are, and so there is no more guilt.

In Reality, nothing has changed or happened. Experiencing is still happening and manifestation is still being perceived. In Reality, nothing has changed or happened, because You have always been the perceiving principle. This is why

> *Enlightenment is best defined as the total conviction that*
> *there is no such thing as enlightenment.*

Paradoxically, the perceiving of manifestation is realized as nothing more than a dream-like apparition in awareness that has no Real significance.

Understand that you are not a seeker or any other object. The Self, likewise, is not an object and so cannot be found or attained, because it is not missing or separate to You.

The concepts of a seeker and some-thing to be sought have spontaneously arisen in awareness, despite you. If you understand this deeply, you will realize 'you' cannot cause these ideas to subside.

There is a story of a farmer who was impatient for his crops to grow. Each night he would go out into his field and tug on the new shoots, hoping they would grow faster.

If any new understandings have come out of all this, don't cling to them. Oftentimes people think that if they keep on reaffirming, "I am not the body," and "There is no such thing as personal will," they will eventually Experience this.

If you tug at the 'new shoots' of understanding in this way, you are much like the farmer in the story. Nothing can be forced, because nothing is in your control. If you try forcing, the idea of control is being more firmly established than ever.

If 'tugging at the new shoots' of your understanding stops, you will find that what you seek has never been separate to you. Unfortunately, 'you' cannot deliberately stop 'tugging' or desiring to know this. This is the seeming dilemma and as it magnifies itself in the mind the desire to know the Self becomes all-consuming.

Then there is nothing to do but live life as you are already doing. Whether you effort or not these actions are happening despite you. When you think "I should be able to go with the flow," that is the flow you are going with. When you think, "I should try to be in the moment," the moment that thought arises is the moment you are in.

Just Be as you are, doing what is being done, and there you Are. As this understanding deepens, all the minds questions and all its answers show themselves to be futile and empty. You know that no answer can bring you the peace you seek.

When the desire to know the Self is experienced to its fullest extent, nothing else matters. All that matters is the desire to know Self, and this desire consumes all others. It consumes even the desire to Be a certain way. Relatively speaking, this is a huge change.

The 'me' identity is so used to needing control that when it begins to lose definition the change is experienced as traumatic. You feel that you are dying or, as I did, that you have died and for some strange reason are still hanging around.

What is happening is that the false sense of self is 'dying.' When the 'me' sense is totally dispelled, for a while the mind can feel more confused than ever. "How did this happen without me? Where was I?" Once the mind recognizes that what has happened occurred despite it, it turns in its habitual circles for a while, but eventually it gives up totally.

This doesn't mean that the mind stops functioning, but that it no longer chases thoughts compulsively. Thoughts that arise subside with equal ease because no-one, no 'me,' is identified with them. Gradually they even arise with less frequency.

Remember these words are just a collection of empty concepts, as all concepts are. The harder the mind tries to grasp them, the more it discovers they are like words written on air. This is the only benefit that can be gained from reading this: the recognition happens that all understandings are empty, void of any absolute truth.

Lost in her spell,
I named her 'myself'
And adorned her
With madness.
Weighed down, she stumbled
Upon "I Am."

Now she wanders
On the moors of my mind
Seeking the Stranger.
When will she tire of all this?

E.V.

Thoughts flit across
The sky of my mind.
Finding no resting place
Their numbers dwindle.
One by one they fall
And 'I' along with them.
What sweetness this decent
Into oblivion
Where, at last, my heart
Is free to soar.

E.V.

Satsang: What is enlightenment?

When enlightenment 'happens,' there is total conviction
that there is no such thing as enlightenment.

PL   *What does it mean 'to be enlightened?'*
EV   The meaning of the word enlightened is 'free of prejudice.'
Unfortunately to many the word enlightenment has conno-
tations of special and is really misunderstood.

PL   *It's very hard not to think of it as special.*
EV   Yes it's easy to think of a fragile sage, sitting on a dais in
India, with a long white beard. Of course my body hasn't
undergone menopause yet, so the last bit might come true!

PL   *What does it feel like?*
EV   Well, joking aside, first you have to realize that no-one ever
becomes enlightened. Enlightenment is just another concept. All it means is that the pseudo-identity is realized to
be a faulty perception. When, beyond a shadow of a doubt
you Know that you are not a body or any concept, enlightenment 'happens.'

It's rather like having a dream in which you see yourself as
a some-one else. Let's say, that you see yourself as a cat.
While the dream is on-going you act and feel exactly like a
cat, and you purr, climb trees, and catch fish in a stream.
Then the dream ends, and you know that is was just a
dream. There you are, in your bed, and realize you have
been dreaming.

Once you awaken you know, beyond a shadow of a doubt,

that you have never been a cat. Has anything really happened to you?

PL *No, but you can't say the dream didn't happen.*
EV Can you say that the dream was real?

PL *Well it was a dream, so it's relatively real.*
EV It's relative only in relation to the one who experiences dreaming. But is the one dreaming different from the one who is awake?

PL *Well, I was in a different state of consciousness while I was dreaming.*
EV Were you unconscious, without any life in you?

PL *No, I didn't stop living.*
EV How was perceiving of the dream possible?

PL *Because of me. Because I am alive.*
EV So, even though, in the dream, you thought 'I Am a cat,' you still had the sense 'I Am.'

PL *Yes.*
EV Then you awaken and the sense 'I Am' is still there. So, what has changed?

PL *Well, in the dream I thought 'I Am a cat.' When I am awake I realize 'I Am a person.'*
EV Either way there is an identity you attach to 'I Am.' In the dream there was one identity and awake there is another identity. But what hasn't changed is the sense 'I Am,' has it?

PL *No.*
EV Essentially then, the change has only affected your sense of identity. It hasn't affected your sense of being, merely the sense of what you *thought* you were.

PL *Yes.*

EV In the first stage of so-called enlightenment, identification with the body stops. You know that you are not the body, and not the mind.

PL *Is this what John writes of as the buddhi stage?*
EV Yes, it is sometimes called that. Buddhi means intellect, and the intellect until then interpreted the reflection of the body to Be 'you.' When the understanding happens that you are not the body the 'split' of the mind can be said to be healing. This stage is one that is helpful to understand, because many people go in and out of it. It's a flip-flopping between identifying with the body and knowing you are not it.

PL *Why? Once you know you are not the body, how would that idea come back and be validated?*
EV During that stage actions happen spontaneously, free of any censorship. This gives the sense of tremendous freedom. As a result there is bliss and gratitude. Suddenly you feel liberated from all the rigid rules you have had for yourself until then.

PL *That must feel incredible.*
EV Yes, it does. The trouble is, because there is such bliss, the mind can easily think 'you' have achieved something. This is why people go in and out of this stage.

Sometimes there isn't a conscious understanding, such as 'I Am not the body.' There is just a deep sense of freedom and actions are efficient, and spontaneous.

Whether a person has a distinct realization or not, the bliss or relief that accompanies this stage is easy to covet. That is, you don't want it to stop.

PL *That would be for sure.*
EV First you must understand that there are no Real 'stages' of enlightenment, or levels. There is a *relative* process that occurs. So, one could say that there is a process of enlightenment, but it describes relative changes only.

For example, there are stages of waking and sleeping. There is deep sleep, when there is no awareness of self. Then there is dreaming, and in a dream you may even think you are awake.

PL *Yes, I've had that experience.*

EV Then you may wake up, but still think you are dreaming. Then you know that you are awake.

The buddhi stage is rather like dreaming and thinking you're awake. My experience was that it was an altered-state. It is often experienced as very blissful. But, this doesn't mean that the other identities have completely fallen away. This is because you feel bliss and gratitude. One feels tremendous gratitude toward everyone and, in particular, toward God and/or one's guru. To feel gratitude you have to feel it in relation to some-one, or some-thing else. This means that there is still a sense of 'me' and 'others.'

PL *So you know you aren't a body, but you still experience separateness?*

EV If you feel deep gratitude there has to be a 'separateness' or some-one to feel gratitude towards. But, deep love and gratitude certainly don't contain painful feelings of separateness. There is a sense of a strong bond or link if you have such feelings towards some-one isn't there?

PL *Yes.*

EV So, in the buddhi stage you feel tremendous gratitude. I always lived rather a hermit's life and tended to spend a great deal of time alone. In the buddhi stage, my husband John, who used to call me anti-social, was amazed. I would take the dogs for a walk in the morning, meet a total stranger and be inviting them home for coffee. This was pretty amazing to me too. I just felt such deep love and gratitude toward life and people in general.

Now if a person entering buddhi believed 'enlightenment'

meant a blissful altered state, they may take the buddhi experience to mean they have 'attained.' Bliss is a word that is so often used to denote enlightenment isn't it?

PL *Yes. In so many teachings, bliss is referred to.*

EV Well if this misunderstanding precedes the buddhi stage it is easy to covet the experience. People begin thinking, "I Am enlightened, and this bliss is the sign." What isn't understood is that some-one is experiencing the bliss. Some-one is involved with the idea of 'attaining' some-thing.

PL *I don't understand.*

EV Remember my explanation at the outset. The word enlightened means 'without prejudice.' Another word for prejudice is impartiality or dispassion. This really describes the absence of desires and needs.

It someone is coveting an experience or taking pride in having 'attained' something, would that describe impartiality or non-involvement?

PL *No. There's strong partiality towards bliss and attainment (laughing).*

EV Yes, that's right. Now, if who you Really are Is infinite, and this is the Knowing, beyond a shadow of a doubt, why would the idea of attaining be there? You already Are every-thing.

PL *Mmm, I see what you mean.*

EV The buddhi stage gives you a sense of detachment. You feel beyond the limitations you had experienced until that point. In the buddhi stage, you feel detached from the body. That gives you such a feeling of freedom—to no longer feel 'confined' to or by the body.

PL *So, what happens then?*

EV Well, if the one in buddhi begins taking pride in the experience, immediately the pseudo-personality, with all its limitations, is turning back towards limitation. The person wants to hold onto the feelings. The bliss is considered personal, and even though the body is no longer identified with, the personality is still strong. The personality wants to be special, feel it has attained.

Freedom is experienced, and as soon as it is considered personal it is limited. Right there in freedom, limitation returns. The personality is still not beyond dualistic concepts. Freedom is thought only possible as long as limitation is absent. This misperception then overrides the buddhi stage and the person experiences 'losing the bliss.'

PL *And you say this happens to lots of people?*
EV Yes. Throughout your lifetime you go in and out of buddhi. This happens especially when you are a child. Of course, not everyone understands the dynamics, or recognizes the dis-identification with the body. Buddhi happens often when you are in love, or buoyed by an experience in which you have let down all your facades.

PL *So, as the facades have only gone temporarily, they can come back just as easily.*
EV Yes, if the feelings that arise are personalized, taken pride in, and coveted. Then the one personalizing them adds them to his or her repertoire of achievements. When this happens the ego can actually become more rigid.

PL *What is the ego exactly, in the way you are talking about it?*
EV Well in psychoanalytical teachings the ego is broken into various categories. What I am talking about when I use the word ego is the sense of presence or being. At first, in what is called the pure ego stage, this sense of presence is impersonal. You could call it the pre-personalized ego. At that point there are no words being used to describe it.

Then the knowledge 'I Am' happens. The sense 'I Am some-thing' follows and the word ego then denotes the personalized sense of presence.

Once identification with the objective world—body, mind,

actions—becomes strong one could say this is the 'un-healthy' ego.

It is a misconception that the ego disappears when 'awak-ening' happens. As long as you have a body, there has to be some identification with it, or who would pee, who would walk?

PL *I wondered about that. So, would you say that you still have an ego?*

EV Yes. I still know that this is my body and that it is different to yours. The difference is that I am identified *with* it, not *as* it. That is a big difference. The ego is just a concept, but one could say that your ego is still relatively unhealthy, whereas mine is healthy.

PL *O.K., I see that. Now if I were to go into buddhi, and didn't covet the bliss, would my ego get healthier? (laughing)*

EV Well let's forget about the ego, because it is a much misun-derstood word. People often think the ego means an over-inflated sense of self. They think the ego, in general, is a bad thing and something to be got rid of. It's just a term, but let's leave it out for now—not to add yet another concept.

PL *O.K.*

EV If bliss and gratitude are enjoyed, but not coveted, the buddhi stage may progress. That is gradually, or quickly, the 'me' personality begins to unravel.

PL *But, you still have a personality.*

EV Interaction is still necessary, as long as there is a body. The way in which interaction happens will be unique, from one body to another. Through each body a unique way of interacting happens. This is called the individuality, the personality. So, yes, I am still interacting and therefore there is a personality.

But the personality that expresses now isn't the contrived one of the 'me.' It's totally impersonal.

RF *But you still recognize that your personality is different to mine or Jake's?*

EV To a degree I still see a difference, although that difference is less distinct to me. Because there isn't any comparing and judging any more, relative distinctions—such as personalities—are really not perceived in the same way they used to be.

If the buddhi experience isn't clung to, the process continues. Gradually the contrived personality, with all its personalized roles, continues to dissolve. What may happen then is what John calls the first stage of Self-realization.

LS *Is Self-realization different to enlightenment?*

EV There are so many schools of thought on this. I don't really relate to stages or to the words, so let's keep it as simple as we can, eh? What may be helpful to you is to understand the relative process. That is all that I'm communicating here. I'm talking about the relative, NOT the Real. Reality, by definition, is unchanging. I'm simply referring to relative changes, not real ones.

LS *Yes, I understand.*

EV In buddhi there can be a strong sense of disorientation from the body. My experience was almost of parallel worlds. There was the sense of detatched witnessing, and there was my body and the rest of the objective world. It was quite disorienting.

LS *When did this happen to you?*

EV I went to see Ramesh about six years ago. At that time the deepest knowing happened that, 'nothing mattered.' It was amazing, and lasted for weeks. Then depression set in and all that mattered was that nothing mattered!

One could say that awakening began there in Bombay, in front of Ramesh. I didn't recognize it as such, and as the feeling deepened the mind became totally confused.

PL *I've heard people say that a 'dark night of the soul' pre*

198

cedes enlightenment. Is this always the case?

EV It does appear to be so in many cases, from what I have heard. It makes sense too, because the mind is used to thinking it should care. When the idea 'nothing matters,' enters the mind, it often interprets this as a negative attitude.

Retrospectively, I recognize that the depression happened, in direct relation to the dissolving of personality habits. When someone has depression, they lose the ability to interact as they used to. They just don't 'feel themselves.' This was exactly how it felt, because the self I had *thought* I was—the 'me'—was disappearing.

PL *Yes. I've suffered a few times from depression. Then nothing—and no-one—seems to be able to stop the sense of isolation.*

EV In this case, I spent most of the two years of depression alone. John was away traveling, but I was relieved not to have anyone around. Although I battled against it sometimes, much of time I just sunk into the 'tunnels' and waited them out. I didn't have to interact, and so could experience the depression fully.

RM *What stopped it?*

EV It stopped spontaneously, in exactly the same way it had come. That is always the case with depression, even though so-called 'reactive depression' seems to have a specific cause.

What happened first was that I sat down and began writing poetry, and then a book. While I wrote the book it absorbed 'me' totally.

PL *What did you write about?*

EV Do you know the word ontology?

PL *No.*

EV Ontology means the investigation of being. The book was really my process of investigating being. I did this by means of my version of jnana yoga—the investigation of concepts. Well, my version of jnana yoga. I investigated every concept that people think of as significant, such as control, sin, enlightenment, illusion.

PL   *What was it called? Did you have it published? Can we read it?*

EV I entitled it *WHO?Cares*. Recently Ramesh actually put out a new book of the same title. It did seem like the perfect title. No, I didn't have it published. I now recognize that the writing was just the process necessary for what was happening. The personality, the 'me' idea, was dissolving, along with all its concepts. The writing was, I guess, the mind's way of explaining the dissolution of dualistic thinking.

But I didn't think anything was happening to me. In fact, I couldn't understand how I could write so clearly and still be 'asleep,' as it were.

Once it was written, and a friend of mine read it, she asked me if there was still a 'me.' By then a lot of weird phenomena had begun happening in my body. When she asked this question, I at first emphatically denied having lost the 'me' sense.

MW *But, wouldn't it be very obvious.*

EV Well, my teacher, Wendell, in London had written saying, "The disappearance of the 'me' is only recognized in retrospect." I didn't believe this at the time. I figured if I woke up one morning and Esther wasn't there any more I'd immediately say, "Thank God!"

But think of it this way. Before you know you have been dreaming, you have to wake up, don't you? Before you can know you are not the cat in your dream, you have to wake up.

MW *Yes.*

EV It is exactly the same when spiritual 'awakening' occurs.

The 'me' 'disappears,' and only then do you realize that you have never been *it*.

You must understand this. The 'me' is the false self—an illusion—un-real. This faulty perception cannot be recognized by the 'me.' That's because it *is* the faulty perception. The cat you think you are in a dream has to disappear before you remember who you are. The cat doesn't realize it isn't you.

RS   *Ah, I see. Who we think we are is an illusion. We can only know this when the illusion has disappeared, is that it?*

EV   The illusion is seen for what it is—just an illusion. The 'me' is just an idea. It's not real. A rope, which is mistaken for a snake, has never been a snake. Therefore, the snake doesn't have to disappear, because it has never existed. What has to happen is a change in perception. The recognition that there is a faulty perception of what is.

RS   *Yes, I get it.*

EV   The illusion of the 'me', is thought of as real. The trouble is, this pseudo-identity wants to—and thinks it can—awaken. Awakening can only happen when the 'me' is gone. It hasn't actually 'disappeared,' because it never had any real existence.

The 'me' is relative to the perceiving principle. The Self is identified with the object, and then, when awakening occurs, this identification ceases. The Self has undergone no *real* change through all this. Any changes are only relative ones.

This is why you must be clear, that all this talk of stages of enlightenment is a relative explanation only. Nothing has *really* happened.

LL   *So who awakens?*

EV   Precisely no-one. If you go to bed and dream you are battling for your life, you have to wake up before you can know that the battle was just a dream.

MW *But sometimes, after dreams like that you feel as if you have been fighting a battle. You wake up exhausted and sweating.*

EV Yes, you do. But has the sense of *being* stopped because of this? Isn't the sense of *being* necessary for both the dreaming and the waking states to happen?

MW *Yes.*

EV A method actor is someone who lets the identity he is playing take the place of his own identity. That is, he totally loses himself in the role. Then, when he comes out of that role, he remembers his own identity. Many method actors say that this stage is very difficult.

You are rather like method actors. You have lost touch with your true identity. It's hidden beneath all the pseudo-identities you've spent your lifetime acting out.

When the buddhi stage happens, suddenly you know you aren't the body. Because you've become so used to thinking 'I Am some-thing,' this habit doesn't necessarily fall away completely, or all in one go.

As an illustration, let's say you're a method actor who's playing *all* the parts in a play. In your two main roles you are a body and a mind. The other roles represent your personality—you play a business-man, a father, and a husband, etc.

At one point you suddenly remember that the two main roles you have been identified as, aren't you. Suddenly you know you aren't the body or mind. This is the so-called buddhi stage.

However, you don't automatically dis-identify from your other roles—the business-man, the husband, the father.

The personality is still strong in the first stage of buddhi. All that has happened is that your primary identity, the body-mind, is recognized as not being You. Of course, this isn't all 'set in stone.' It really varies a lot from case to case.

LL *So, if the personality is still strong, this is why it might still identify with its roles? This is why it might cling to the role of enlightenment?*

EV Yes. If the personality is still strong and pride comes in, this is when the buddhi experience stops. If this doesn't happen, gradually, the 'me' subsides fully.

TM *Is this the 'I Am' stage John writes about?*

EV I don't relate to demarcations too well in all this. But, with the depersonalization of the personality, the ideas, 'I Am a business-man,' 'I Am a father,' fall away. You still use those labels in everyday language to describe what you are doing. The difference is that you aren't identified with any role.

Then there is just the sense 'I Am' with no labels attached to it anymore. In this stage there is no longer the experience of parallel worlds. It can almost seem as if something has been lost. This is because the sense of a witness, or parallel worlds has stopped.

Remember, I'm not describing *all* cases. The experience varies according to the physical mechanism through which it is experienced.

When the 'I Am' stage 'happens,' a sense of limbo can result, and the idea 'I Am neither this nor that,' is there. This can again be a time when depression happens. The body and mind are used to playing out within the framework of being some-thing. Actually, it's more like a faint grieving. The mind is grieving an old way of being.

LL *So, the mind is still active?*

EV At this stage the mind can still be very active. It can even seem as if the mind is more active than ever. The mind is trying to figure out "How did this happen without 'me'?' But you are no longer identified with the mind and so these thoughts arise and subside in quick succession. It feels almost as if the mind is channel surfing.

Until then, thoughts are horizontal—you think in terms of

beginnings and endings. Then suddenly they are being vertically cut off. In this stage the cutting off of thoughts feels very odd. The radical change in the mind's way of functioning takes a while to get used to. A thought arises and suddenly it's gone. No thoughts are pursued as they used to be.

TM *It sounds a bit like Alzheimer's.*
EV Well, from what I know, Alzheimer's patients are totally absorbed by what is going on at the moment. Nothing is compared to past experiences or related to outcome. This is how the 'I Am' stage is experienced too. The difference might be that the Alzheimer's patient becomes very disturbed if someone suddenly intrudes on what is happening.

In 'I Am', whatever is being witnessed has total focus. If a new element enters into the experience, this is also witnessed. There is no sense of disturbance, and no agitation occurs.

TM *Ah, O.K.*
EV In the 'I Am,' or what is called the first level of Self-realization, there is still a possibility of 'coming out' of it. The personality habits can still re-engage.

TM *Did you experience going 'in and out' of these stages?*
EV No, I didn't have that sense. It was simply a progressive deepening or stabilizing. Dispassion deepened and with it the sense of peace. I didn't have a sense of coming out of it, but rather that it was a continuous deepening.

LL *So the buddhi witnessing stage must feel like an altered state, does it?*
EV Yes, I felt it as a strong altered state. This is what made it clear that an aspect of the 'me' still had to be there. Someone was experiencing the altered state and enjoying it.

My sense is that the extreme disorientation from the body helped to anchor the relative process. It isn't always like that. John didn't have this sense of it at all.

Sometimes in the buddhi stage there is the sense, 'I Am That.' If prior teachings gave the idea of a 'you' and Source, it can be thought that, 'I Am That' refers to Source. What is probably the case is the Witness is being identified with, and 'I Am That' is actually the mind relating to the Witness. The mind's habit of interpreting, relative to prior programming, is still strong then.

TM   *Once one stabilizes in 'I Am,' what happens then?*
EV   Gradually the limbo stage of not being 'this or that' was like an expanding emptiness. I could only describe it as a 'sweet' emptiness.

Now I really can't put words to any of it. It's just totally familiar and natural, whereas the 'me' was clearly an altered state and quite unnatural. So it's very clear that nothing has happened to Me. Nothing has *really* happened.

I remember feeling so surprised at the subtlety and naturalness. The mind was still expecting a radical change. The 'me' sense is far from subtle.

As the mind is being cut off, and actions are spontaneous and uncensored, it feels like being a tiny child again. It all feels so natural.

LL   *It's hard not to think of enlightenment as a dramatic*
       happening.
EV   Yes. The connotation of specialness isn't one that falls away easily. When the naturalness and subtlety is recognized, you think, "Well, of course, this is who I Really am, so why would it feel special or unnatural, or like an altered-state?"

If you compare the 'me' experience to the present experience the change IS dramatic. But you see, once the 'me' falls away it's hard to relate back to it as having happened at all. It becomes like a very faint memory or someone else. The relative changes are dramatic, but there is no-one left to really appreciate them.

The physical changes are enjoyable, but if the 'me' would

have been able to experience them it would have been ecstatic. That's why Ramesh used to say, "If you are offered a million dollars or enlightenment, take the million dollars. Because when enlightenment happens there is no-one there to enjoy it."

TM *Mmm, I sort of 'get' it, but it's hard.*
EV Yes, the pseudo-identity doesn't 'get' it really, because it doesn't want to. It likes to believe 'it' can 'attain enlightenment.' This idea is, paradoxically, what sets the seeking in motion and keeps it going—until the mind does 'get' that it can never understand the truth of You.

TM *So now what do you feel like?*
EV Very natural and absolutely ordinary is the best way of describing it. All desires to be other than I am have gone. The desire to become special, has dissolved in ordinariness.

When I was 'cornered into' satsang, the paradox hit me. I realized it would be fairly impossible for me to talk about these things without others thinking of me as special. Here I was, finally feeling wonderfully ordinary, and taking on a role that would possibly set me apart in others' eyes.

TM *Well, it is hard not to think of you as very different to us.*
EV It will be good when you begin coming here and recognizing, albeit intellectually, that there is no essential difference.

When this understanding is there, the mind gets out of the way, and listening is total. Self is communing with Self.

And the word Self, or Atman, gives a misunderstanding too. I guess you could say it's all just Consciousness at play within itself. Listening, talking, communing.

LL *Are you still in the 'I Am' stage?*
EV No. The 'Amness' or sense of substance has totally disappeared. 'Amness' describes the emotions and memories stored in the body. The ones you suppress because they

hurt or you think they are inappropriate.

You see you are born with natural characteristics, unique to your bodymind. The pseudo-personality judges these traits and embellishes on some, and rejects others. Then the Amness becomes dense and the density is these 'holdings.' Retrospectively, I realize that there was a physical denseness. Now the body feels so different, so light.

When the false personality falls away, what remains are the innate characteristics you were born with. This means that both negative and positive traits express themselves, without censorship, dynamically.

PL *Ah, so that means you aren't suddenly a 'perfect' person.*
EV Exactly. What you would once have called imperfections, are no longer censored. Self-expression is impersonal, so who is there to censor anything and why?

The mind has so many preconceived notions about enlightenment. One of these notions is that enlightenment will make you 'perfect.' Of course perfections and imperfections are mere judgments. And the idea of perfection varies from person to person.

When there is no-one to judge, dualistic thinking ceases. The funny thing is that for a while—in the 'I Am' stage— the mind can still get into judging and interpreting the lack of judgment. This is why people can go in and out of that stage too. The mind hasn't ceased all involvement.

LL *So it's all paradox after paradox.*
EV Yes. During the process from buddhi to Self-realization the recognition of paradox deepens.

What I didn't mention about the buddhi stage was perhaps the most dramatic *relative* change I experienced: until then I had spent my life feeling the world was hostile. I thought I was experiencing everyone else's emotions and pains. Clearly, 'others' were simply a reflection of the emotional holdings in my own body.

MW I have tremendous problems with that too. I've always been hyper sensitive to my surroundings.

EV In this phenomenon the person experiencing it is often referred to as 'a sensitive.' The alternative is a numbing-off to the world, or more accurately, a total numbing off to one's emotional holdings.

MW Sometimes I think I'd rather be numbed off.

EV Yes, it can be devastating. I've always been amazed at people who actually do workshops to develop this sensitivity. I always considered it a curse. But people are fascinated by phenomena. As if the phenomenal experience of the body as self isn't enough. To that people add all manner of other weird and wonderful phenomena.

They actually go out of their way to add to their dilemma. Then they think they are 'more spiritual,' or 'more aware.' All the while they never bother to ask, "How is the experiencing of anything possible?"

It's easy in the first stages to be distracted by phenomena, because there can be many. Dizziness, nausea, disorientation, strange body sensations, etc.

I suddenly realized that the phenomenon that surprised me most was that I no longer experienced anyone in my environment. This makes sense, of course, because there is no 'other' to experience. I guess this cessation wasn't a phenomenon, but actually the absence of one.

MW Good. It's nice to know it might stop one day.

EV If you understand what is happening at such times, don't give it any undue attention. Just recognize it for what it is and don't struggle against it or become involved in the feelings. When you keep a perspective on it, it helps a lot.

But, as long as there are emotional holdings in the body, that experience will probably carry on. In this case, the tension that left the body when the 'me' sense dissolved was amazing. Then all other residual 'holdings' began to dissolve too.

On and off, for a week, I would experience various emotions. That is, I didn't experience them in the 'normal' way. In Chinese medicine it is taught that all the emotions have corresponding organs and body aspects. Much of your life the emotions are either in excess or in deficiency. This means that instead of stimulating the healthy functioning of their corresponding organs, the imbalanced emotions cause excess, or deficient conditions in the related body aspects.

What happened was that, on and off, for a couple of weeks, I would have a clear sense of fear, but it wasn't experienced in the way an emotion usually is. .

I just knew there was fear, or grief, but can't say I 'had' the emotions. It was as if they sat over the heart for a while. Then they moved to the solar plexus, and then the intestines would gurgle and the emotion would dissolve. This happened for quite a few days.

PT *But, emotions were still there afterwards?*
EV I still experience emotions, but they aren't related to past memories. Emotions can still arise in relation to what is, but they have nothing to do with the surfacing of old baggage or 'holdings.' There is no pneumonic or memory factor accompanying any emotions now.

It's the bodymind's nature to react to stimuli. Your reactions are triggered by the (memory) holdings in your body. These holdings and the momentary reaction come together, and over-reaction happens.

When these 'holdings' dissolved in my body it seemed to get lighter and lighter. This had nothing to do with weight loss. The sense of density just disappeared. Now over-reactions just don't happen.

JV I used to practice astral traveling. Clearly, no-one leaves the body then, but the sense is that you leave it. I remember when I used to 'come back into' the body, it felt like heavy, wet clay. It was a horrible sensation.

EV Yes. We don't realize the sense of density that emotional holdings give to the body. I'm sure if I weighed three hundred pounds right now, the body would still not be experienced as heavy and dense.

When this emotional holding dissolved, it helped me understand the reason we have eating disorders. We are always feeding—or starving—those emotional holdings. It's the only way we can keep them there.

Relatively speaking, the changes that occurred in the body once the emotional holdings dissolved were dramatic. The long-term health problems I had, due to neuro-toxic poisoning, disappeared. The body became, almost overnight, healthier, more vital, and continues to experience good health. When ailments occur, they remedy themselves really quickly.

JV In my studies and teaching of bioenergetics, it has been fascinating to watch this process. What happened with Esther's body is very much in line with bioenergetic theory. It is just rare to see it in action in such a dynamic way.

LL *But you still react to situations?*

EV The body and mind can still react, which is natural to them. The difference is each situation is experienced as if for the first time. That is, there's no regurgitating of past similar situations. There are no emotional memory holdings. This means that the reaction is fully felt toward the situation. Anger, grief or joy, might arise, but because it's not censored, it's experienced fully and subsides as fast as it came.

LL *In what I've read of enlightenment, I always got the im pression it just happened, poof, all in one go.*

EV Do remember that no-one ever 'gets' enlightened. Enlightenment, or impartiality, is the natural state. The unnatural state is simply recognized for what it is. This 'recognition' is a relative process that happens in stages. Enlightenment really describes the relative process of the falling away of

210

involvement. It doesn't describe anything Real.

But yes, I too had the idea it was a one-up thing, poof, and that was it. And maybe in some cases it is. That's how most have written about it that I've read. When people ask me, 'when did you awaken,' I can't say on such and such a day at such and such a time. I can say that the relative process began in front of Ramesh.

LL   *Would you say you are 'fully enlightened' then.*

EV   No. I consider 'full enlightenment' to be very rare. Shankara of the North, and I think there is one in the south, and Sri Nisargadatta Maharaj—just before he died— are what I considered embodiments of the 'fully enlightened.'

LL   *But you would still say you are 'awake.'*

EV   I no longer am identified as being the body or any object or concept. I'm no longer living under any delusion. So in this sense I'm 'awake,' yes.

It is now clear that there has never been a seeker or a Sought. There had always only been impersonal seeking, doing, seeing, listening. All there Is, is Consciousness, or Experiencing.

At this point the, 'Amness,' or false personality has completely disappeared. Now one could say the 'I,' or individuality remains identified with Experiencing or manifest-Self.

Just when I thought all questions had ceased, the question arose, "What is the Source of Experiencing?" "What is the perceiving principle of the 'I'?"

LL   *So, even then there are still questions.*

EV   Yes, this question suddenly arose. I understood that the Atman or Self is not separate to the Absolute—not-two. But the Absolute was not a direct awareness. I guess there was the expectation that this all happened 'poof' all at once.

Anyway, then even the natural disposition began to lose definition—although I didn't have an immediate recognition of this. The mind seems to be turning further 'inward' as it were. Now there are no more questions.

TM *So, isn't that the end of the process?*
EV No. In some rare cases while the body is still alive, the individuality dissolves to but a faint trace. This is when 'I Am' consciousness, body, mind and all duality are 'transcended.' This describes the embodiment of Sat-guru.

LL *But isn't that like being a vegetable then?*
EV No, not at all. But let me explain individuality a little better. Through each body, Consciousness expresses in different ways. This expression is called individuality. It's still all Consciousness, just manifesting in various ways.

As long as there is a body via which interaction and experiencing happens, a 'tune' has to be played. Interaction has to continue. The sage still pees, eats, drinks, and walks. Therefore, a modicum of personality must remain, for all this to continue happening.

Every-one is 'born' with unique traits or a unique disposition—individuality. Until you begin interacting with the world this individuality could be said to be neutral. When interaction begins individuality becomes more animated and loses its neutrality.

LL *So are you saying that when individuality dissolves it's more childlike, or more like the newborn infant?*
EV It would have the gentleness that precedes the dynamism of interaction. It certainly doesn't describe a 'vegetable' state. Nisargadatta (Maharaj), was one of the rare Sat-gurus and from what I have seen of videos of him he certainly didn't fit the description of 'vegetable.'

I can only talk from my own, present experience. The best way I would describe it is that there is a gentling process—although I know there isn't such a word. This 'gentling' process happens as the individuality loses it's habits of interaction. If the habits are very strong, religious, social, whatever, it may be very gradual. But it's all just ongoing, spontaneous *relative* changes with no-one to be concerned about them.

MW *So would you say you are in the process of Sat-guru?*
EV You know, it's all just words and labels. I don't relate to *any* of them. But once the Jnani stage 'happens' one could say the dissolution of individuality begins happening to some degree or other in all cases.

Now that all the labels have fallen away it seems everyone is more interested in labeling me. It's so strange. All I can say is that there is a *relative* ongoing process. This process varies from case to case.

In some cases, individual self-expression undergoes only small changes during the remaining existence of the body. If the awakening process was preceded by particularly strong cultural beliefs, or spiritual beliefs they may not subside much at all, or very gradually.

I.L *So all belief systems don't fall away?*
EV There are still beliefs, but they are impersonal. It's not the same as before when the beliefs were personal agendas, 'this is how it is!'

They can still come across that way sometimes, but that's just from the perspective of someone listening. The beliefs are impersonal. But they do color the way in which interaction happens, especially where teaching is concerned. Many continue to teach from the standpoint of their cultural and social backgrounds.

Some teach yogic postures are necessary. They know that awakening happens spontaneously, but their own process included *asanas* (yoga postures) and other disciplines, so they continue teaching them as if they are a prerequisite to awakening.

Others may have followed a pathway involving abstinence and rituals. They teach from the standpoint of self-control. Even though they Know that there is no such thing as control, they teach from the perspective of their own process prior to awakening. So, do understand, communication can still be colored by mental filters. It's easy to take everything the guru says as gospel truth. Don't believe anything. No words ever hold absolute truth. The words of the guru can point you away from the false self, but if teachings are colored by rigid beliefs they may not even be that helpful.

In such cases it's the 'being in the presence' of 'one' who embodies impersonal Consciousness that can trigger the shifts, rather than what they are teaching.

LL   *Makes me wonder, why would you want to teach?*
EV   Well, if it happens it happens. In my case I was teaching before and so teaching continued. It's no more or less significant than any other action.

LL   *You seem to talk more animatedly about some things than others.*
EV   It's all just an impersonal functioning, like ripples on a pond. Sometimes the ripples are more like waves, but they all subside into neutrality.

MW *Isn't it hard to keep on writing and talking if the mind is so peaceful?*
EV   Well, I have written prolifically all my life whereas I was always more of a hermit when it came to interacting. So writing is still easier than talking. But, I have to say words almost overwhelm me lately. Just words, words, words. But writing spews out and it's almost a relief to write.

MW *So is your mind still active?*
EV   When I'm writing it's active, but very peaceful and thoughts are effortless. I don't really have a perspective on the changes. I guess I've got used to them. But I am notic-

ing that when interaction is necessary, it's often rather like coming up to the top of a deep ocean. The mind is really very peaceful, and that is its nature, after all. You weren't born with a stressed-out mind. So sometimes it's almost hard to interact.

JV Yes, to me there are dramatic changes. Sometimes it can almost be annoying, but it is more funny than annoying. She begins doing something and then is so easily distracted. I guess, as no action is considered important, it's easy to be distracted.

I watch Esther when the mind is still, and when she has to interact it's almost as if it's an effort. It's as if she has to pull herself out of stillness and effort to create personality waves. I notice that it is increasingly 'difficult' for her to create the Esther personality to interact with me.

EV Yes, now John refers to me as the perfect blonde—the mind's almost empty!

JV On the whole the changes are wonderful. She still can get angry, although that's rare. When it happens though, the anger is strong. Then, as quick as it came, it's, gone as if nothing has happened.

It makes life very easy, because I don't have to act in a certain way any more. I don't have to pre-meditate her reactions.

EV And, because you are also in this 'process' John, you don't really have the sense of needing to act a certain way either do you?

JV No.

LL *You said, most teach according to their own background, whatever their process was before awakening.*
EV Yes.

LL *So, how do you define the way in which you teach?*
EV Well my process was my form of jnana yoga. I investigated

concepts, and beliefs, with a view to discovering, or un-covering, the paradox of concepts. I figured that my mind was too active to meditate, although Reiki is perhaps the truest meditation because the mind cuts itself off during it. When one self-treats, there is no effort to achieve anything. So, for fifteen years I did practice Reiki.

Other than Reiki, I didn't relate to other forms of medita-tion. As my mind was sharp, I decided to use the power of discrimination constructively. I investigated and unraveled concepts and beliefs.

This is what you experience when you are here and in Breakthrough. I don't let you get away with any concepts. Anything you say is investigated, until you realize it con-tains no absolute truth.

PT   *Yup, you take no prisoners. It can be very frustrating, but I keep on coming back. Guess I'm a masochist.*

EV   Don't you keep on coming back because you are experienc-ing more peace of mind, more peace?

PT   *Yes, there's confusion, but it seems to clear out so much baggage, that then there's peace.*

MW *So, what happens when most of the individuality is gone or at minimum?*

EV   When the individuality has lost most of its 'strength' the mind turns fully inward as it were. Until then manifest-Self is the Knowing, but then I Am-Consciousness and duality is transcended and the Absolute is simply awareness. And I can only talk on this from what is deeply intuited.

LL   *But how can the manifest-Self experience the non-mani fest?*

EV   That is not what I'm saying. Understand that they are not-two. There is no-one experiencing the Atman or manifest-Self. The intellect is an expression of consciousness. It registers the Knowing but does not understand it.

When individuality dissolves to but a trace, it's said that there is but a 'flicker' of movement in the mind.

This whole 'process' is rather like moving from the circumference of a wheel to its hub—the still point. The mind, body and manifest-Consciousness—or I Am-consciousness are 'transcended.'

Of course no-one transcends any-thing. But this describes the embodiment of Sat-guru or 'full enlightenment'—it's all just words and more words. It's so easy to get hung up on them all.

In this case the experiential state of being (minus labels) is what is happening. The relative process is therefore incomplete. Understand, I'm only talking here of a relative process—nothing real.

Your only concern right now is to discover who you are not. This is the first 'stage,' Knowing 'I Am' without all the labels—'I Am' without words. I talk about Sat-guru because it must be understood that consciousness without words is only the first 'stage.'

'I Am consciousness' ceases at the death of the body, so you can only Be that which preceded it. The perceiving principle of it, which is termed the Absolute, para-Brahman, para-Atman—there are many terms.

Just remember that I have only described relative happenings, nothing Real. What is Real cannot be put into words, so don't cling to words. Perhaps we have dispelled some old ways of thinking. If that's the case, it's good. Don't think of any of this as important. It is just 'descriptions,' not 'prescriptions.' Perhaps it will serve to point your focus away from the pseudo-identity just a little bit more.

Silence

Of the pregnant Silence
No-thing is born.
No-one hears the words
That fill It,
And no words can describe
The Silence they fill.
Broken by noise,
Silence is undestroyed.
Born of Itself,
No-thing is created.
When noise subsides
Into Silence
What has changed?
Nothing has happened.

E.V.

How do you know that you are?

Q.   *After Self-realization there is no-one left to be interested in the next stage is there?*

A.   No. Remember these stages are just relative happenings, nothing real. The goal-oriented 'me' is gone. No Self has been realized and no-one realized it. Nothing has ever happened or will happen that will affect Me. There is just impersonal functioning, but it is still happening in a unique way through this body. This is what we call the individuality—the essential nature.

While individuality is still fairly well-defined, the love of being is still there, oriented to the body.

Now there is an ongoing relative process. Dispassion or neutrality is deepening, even toward the love to be.

Q.   *Do you meditate? You talk of focusing on the 'I Am.'*

A.   There are no longer any false identities; so there is no-one to meditate on any-thing. Although one might say that this Is meditation, but not in the generally understood sense.

While 'I Am' is still adorned with labels it's helpful to meditate or focus on it. Then gradually you stop being hypnotized by this and that, and the labels subside.

The 'I' or individuality is, however, still identified with beingness—manifest-Self, or manifest-Consciousness. This experiential state can only happen while the body exists. But both the body and Experiencing are dependent on the non-manifest in which they are reflected.

I am not this 'I,' which will cease when the body dies. I can only Be the perceiving principle of it. But 'awareness' of the perceiving principle is not possible while individuality is still strong. The relative process happening now is the 'neutralizing' of individuality. That may continue until the body dies. It can be minimal, gradual or very fast.

But there's no-one, no pseudo-identity, to have any interest in it. It's just a spontaneous, effortless process.

Q.   *But the sense of Being is still linked to the body?*
A.   Without the body the sense of being wouldn't be possible. There is still identification with the body, but I Am not identified as it. That's a big difference.

Right now you think the body and its roles are you.

I experience being because of this body. And 'I Am' is being expressed in a way that is unique to this particular mechanism.

Q.   *Isn't that still the 'I Am' stage John wrote about?*
A.   No. In the so-called 'I Am' stage the individuality still has strong habits of interaction. These habits are the 'holdings' I talked of. The Amness is a feeling of density consisting of thought/emotions related to the past. It's the accumulation of memories that are held onto and suppressed.

When I say 'I Am' is being expressed in a unique way, I'm talking about the sense of being in relation to this body. No sense of 'Amness' remains, so experiences are no longer colored or distorted by past events. There is a newness to all experiences. This can't happen while the sense of 'Amness' is there.

Q.   *But isn't the individuality to do with a memory?*
A.   It has nothing to do with learned or programmed behavior. At the birth of the body there are in-born traits or individual characteristics. Before interaction begins, individuality is impersonal. When interaction begins, at first, these traits aren't personalized, so they are still expressed spontaneously without censorship. But the demonstration

of individuality in-relation to 'others' marks a relative change in the natural temperament.

Before this happens there is no love of being. There is simply being, without awareness of it in-relation to anything else.

Then the idea comes of 'being a certain way,' in relation to 'others.' Then attachments to those 'others' begin. This is when the idea of 'becoming other than you are' takes hold and the love of being changes.

Sometimes the frustration with not being a certain way is so strong the body is put to an end. If this doesn't happen, the need to become other than you are just keeps on growing—in some more than others.

When the pain of feeling unfulfilled and lacking becomes overwhelming, seeking may begin. Then you want to see beyond all the labels and desires. The desire to know That which preceded all the desires then grows.

Q. *Now all I want is for that desire to stop!*
A. Exactly. That is what turns the mind in upon itself. Rather than thinking in terms of beginnings and endings it finds itself tripping over the desire not to desire Self. Then the circular nature of the mind is recognized. Until then thinking is seen in terms of beginnings and endings.

It's like looking at the movement of a pendulum from side-on. You just see it going back and forth. The mind seems to oscillate between past and future only.

Then you see the 'pendulum' from above and realize it's always just been swinging in circles. This is what the mind has always been doing, turning in circles.

When this is realized the circles seem to get more frenetic as the mind turns in upon itself. As the 'circles' get smaller you realize that the mind keeps on tripping over the same old, same old.

Q.   *It's so painful.*

A.   Yes, and as this pain grows it consumes 'you.' It gradually consumes the pseudo-identity looking to see beyond itself. The mind can seem crazy, or at least you realize that it has always been craziness. This is when the mind may at last give up trying to do anything. When this giving-up is total, Seeing happens beyond dualistic concepts. Then the Knowing is that nothing has ever been personal.

Of course, this isn't the 'process' in all cases. Sometimes, love of the Divine is so pure, so strong, it simply burns away all the facades.

Unfortunately, the western mind has become very complicated and the 'process' isn't always that simple. When the mind's thinking processes are very complex they form a very strong 'covering' of the heart. Then what we call love is far from neutral, it's super conditional.

Q.   *So unconditional love is bullshit then? We can't possibly love unconditionally while the mind is so complicated?*

A.   Yes, most of the time unconditional love is the bullshit that the complicated mind likes to kid itself it is capable of. So unconditional love is aimed for. While the mind is doing the aiming, the heart is rarely unencumbered.

I remember returning from seeing Ramesh and saying to John, "I thought I knew how to love, but now I realize I've never really loved before."

Of course, John then pointed out that "The love you felt in front of Ramesh was nothing to do with worldly love. It was love of the Divine which can't be compared in any way to what you feel for 'others'."

This was clear to me too, but at that time it made even my love for John seem totally deficient. I understood that John was also an expression of the Divine, but I couldn't feel this as I did in front of Ramesh.

Q.   *Now do you experience love of the Divine? Is that the love of the Absolute?*

A.   What is termed the Absolute is the perceiving principle of all this. When love of the Divine is pure, not just a needy love of God-as-a-crutch, it means the mind is out of the way. But there's still a pseudo-identity experiencing this love.

Now that pseudo-self is gone, who's left to love the Divine? No-one.

When 'Amness' fell away there was pleasure in just being. Now there is dispassion, or growing neutrality towards even this beingness. Love, as you think of it, isn't the experience anymore.

Q.   *But you still love John don't you?*

A.   I can't call it love in at all the usual sense. There is a neutrality, an ever-deepening neutrality.

Q.   *Is it a kind of disinterest then?*

A.   Well, I wouldn't call it disinterest, because there is a bond between the bodies called John and Esther. We still nurture each other and there are still practical concerns about each other's welfare. It's also a much stronger link than between any other bodies.

The difference is that there is no dependency. I still make meals and clean the house, and John still earns most of the money. The two bodies still require maintenance and there is still enjoyment at interacting and nurturing one another.

Because neither of us recognizes any real 'other' there is neutrality. Out of this neutrality actions happen that aren't neutral, that demonstrate caring. These actions then subside into neutrality.

Q.   *But there is caring?*

A.   Yes, but it isn't the needy form of 'caring' that happens between two people who think in terms of a 'me' and the 'other.' It is quite impersonal.

Duality has been recognized to be an inter-relationship, a paradox. Within no-thingness this body appears and I experience being because of it. Within no-thingness John's body appears and a bond has formed between these two bodies.

This inter-relationship or relationship is an effect within Consciousness or Reality. But, the Reality which underlies these appearances is unaffected and unchanged by them.

There is the inter-relatedness of the 'I' (individuality) and this body. There is the inter-relatedness of one unique expression of being to another.

Until inter-relatedness or duality is transcended, the relative process of what is called 'enlightenment' is incomplete.

Q. *But who is there to transcend the duality?*
A. That's a good question. There is no 'one' to transcend duality, you're right.

Q. *As there's still a sense that the process is incomplete, is there impatience with this?*
A. No, there is no impatience because there is no-one waiting for or wanting any-thing. There is simply a deepening of dispassion toward this beingness.

The intellect is the expression of consciousness. At first the intellect is fully caught up in the love of being. When individuality is strong the intellect is mesmerized by it. As individuality loses definition the 'spell' it had over the intellect is gradually broken. This can be described by the deepening of dispassion.

In the tiny baby, at first, there is just the impulse to sustain the body. These tendencies are innate, natural, impulses. There aren't any thoughts of 'I want,' 'I don't want.' It's all just the natural instinct of preservation of the beingness. As the child receives more input, the tendency toward more than just basic necessities grows.

Q. *Would you say you still have physical wants?*

A. The instinct to take care of the body is there. I still drink when I feel thirsty. I still eat when I feel hunger. These 'wants' are more practical requirements. But along with practical requirements there is still the tendency to provide the body with things that aren't absolutely necessary.

Much of the time this all happens in the same way it does for a child. A child is attracted toward doing something and then is easily distracted and loses interest.

I begin doing something that isn't vital or necessary and find interest has suddenly waned.

Q. *I've heard it said that the sage is the 'super enjoyer.' What does this mean exactly?*

A. The sage's enjoyment is similar to that of a child. A tiny child enjoys everything because everything is new to it. The tiny child hasn't learned to reject or cling to any experience. Everything, every event, is fully experienced. And, because every experience is new, the child is distracted easily. He fully enjoys one experience until another one presents itself.

It's the same with the sage. To the sage all experiences have a newness, because no experience is colored or distorted by memories. This is what's meant by being a 'super enjoyer.' Censorship and comparing is absent, so everything is fully experienced.

Because your mind has the habit of censoring, nothing is experienced fully. You want this then that, but as soon as you have anything, you are already thinking about the next thing you want. That doesn't describe distractedness. It describes compulsive behavior.

Q. *My little boy has a toy he loves and then he loses interest in it and is asking me for a new bike, or a new pair of skates. He's quickly dissatisfied with things, and always seems to be wanting something new.*

A. Your little boy has already learned the idea of ownership. He's learned the idea of comparison and compares this to

225

that. He probably sees what his friends have and wants the same. That's compulsive behavior.

That brings to mind when I was a little girl and my mother used to make all my clothes. She made me a dress I loved with patterns of sheep all over it and little leg-o-lamb sleeves.

Then one-day we were standing in a store together and I saw a little girl standing next to me with a dress of the exact same fabric. The difference was all her sheep were the right way up. Until that point I hadn't realized my sheep were upside down because when I looked down at my dress they were all the right way up.

I remember tugging at my mother's sleeve, most distressed, saying "Mummy, Mummy all my sheep are dead!" After that I loathed wearing that dress. That was probably when the first sense of self-image and comparing began.

Until that happens the child doesn't have needs. It just enjoys whatever presents itself because it's all so new to it. It's this kind of distractedness I'm talking about when everything is enjoyed but nothing is clung onto or rejected.

Q. *Now though it sounds as if you are rejecting the sense of being?*

A. Again, there is no-one to reject any-thing. I guess if the love of being is dissipating, it might sound as if there is rejection of it. That's just because you still think in terms of love versus hate, or dislike. While this way of thinking persists, emotions swing in extremes.

I no longer think in these terms. The way I would describe it now is that there's a neutralizing of tendencies. The habits of providing unnecessary input are waning.

Orientation within duality is changing. Everything is of decreasing significance, which I'd call a distractedness. With this 'distractedness' the mind is also less active, more peaceful, or impartial.

All my focus as a seeker was to 'realize' being, minus the labels and identities. But beingness, or whatever you want to call it, is dependent on the body and the mind. While orientation is still strong toward this beingness or experiential state there is no direct awareness of the perceiving principle of this beingness. Although I know I am That, the orientation is still towards the functioning happening in relation to duality.

Q. *By 'That' do you mean the Absolute?*
A. Yes. But remember, that's just a word, a concept. By using a noun it's hard not to objectify the *noumenon* (unmanifest). That in which the phenomenal world is reflected cannot be an experiential state.

It is awareness only, aware of awareness. Of course there are no words to describe the non-describable, unnameable. But for the purpose of differentiation, words must be used.

There is no real difference between consciousness and the Absolute. They are not-two. Consciousness or beingness is an expression of the Absolute and so cannot be separate to It. To think of them as separate would be like thinking of wetness as a quality apart from water.

You know how it is when you learn something. First you have an intellectual understanding of it and you think 'now I get it.' You are sure you have a clear understanding.

When you come here you probably leave thinking, "Ah, now I've understood." Then you come back again and are surprised to find the understanding was incomplete. Then you think, "Ah, now I really understand."

Each time you return, the 'understanding' goes a little deeper, so what you thought you understood deeply shows itself to have been only a superficial understanding.

Q. *Yes, I keep on coming and feeling I'm 'getting' it and then find I hadn't got it at all, or only partially.*

A. That is because the 'understanding' is selective. You understand that everything happens despite you and that is a
relief. Then someone does something you dislike, and you
blame them. This shows you that your 'understanding' is
filtered through your beliefs.

When you really 'get' all this you won't come here anymore. There will be nothing to 'get' because you will know
you Are what you were trying to 'get.'

Before the labels were recognized as false, I thought I had a
fairly good understanding. When they 'fell away' it was just
like the difference between learning how to do something
and actually experiencing 'doing' it.

Only once you put theory into practice do you start understanding and seeing the whole picture. You discover that
you hadn't understood completely. The real learning happens through experiencing, not theorizing.

Before I had the theory of 'enlightenment,' I knew the
word only described a relative process, but still there were
so many ideas and expectations about this process.

Once the labels were recognized as false the experiencing
of being minus labels resurfaced.

Q. · *As a tiny child that experience is there isn't it?*
A. Well in the newborn infant there is simply awareness. The
child's mind is innocent and hasn't begun censoring, judging, or comparing.

One of the interpretations of innocent is 'not tainted with
blame.' So it could be said the so-called 'original sin' is
identification with the body. Before this identity begins
being discriminated against and the false self-image grows,
the child's innocence is naïve, unaffected and unsophisti-
cated.

Q. *Isn't that what innocence means: lack of sophistication or
lack of understanding?*
A. There's a lack of knowledge or information about self. The

word innocence comes from the Latin word *innocens,* meaning blameless. Another way of saying blameless would be guilt-free. The tiny child is innocent—free of guilt —because it hasn't started to judge and hasn't yet learned right from wrong.

Q.   *But children do have to learn these differences.*
A.   Yes, this is the progression that happens. The child goes from naïve innocence, not feeling guilt, to learning information about itself and life. This information describes the child to itself, and orients it to 'others.' Then comparing begins and guilt sets in.

Q.   *But this can't be avoided can it? I mean you can't teach a child it isn't its body and that right and wrong are just concepts.*
A.   No, a child has to learn about interaction and relationships. It has to learn what is beneficial and what is harmful. If you have a deep understanding about all this, you may be able to teach the child rather than indoctrinate it.

Q.   *Exactly what is the difference? I kind of understand, but...*
A.   Linguistically there's probably a fine line between the two words. But I'm making a differentiation to serve my point.

When your perspective is relatively free of strong judgments you'll teach a child about the practical concerns of interacting and living in the world. You're less likely to teach from the standpoint of strong personal agendas.

If you are strongly identified with guilt and have a strong moralistic stance, you can only indoctrinate. Then what you teach is colored by your own fears and rigid ideas about good and bad.

This would be a description of indoctrination as I mean it. You are imparting dogma rather than a practical recipe for how to live in the world.

Q.   *But even if you teach rather than indoctrinate a child won't stay innocent.*

A.   No, but it is less likely to grow up with a totally jaded view of the world and itself. It's probably going to grow up demonstrating more wisdom than a child who's indoctrinated. This 'wisdom' is still the result of learning. But it's more the accumulation of practical information, than dogmatic beliefs.

The only purpose of having a body is to go beyond learned information—be it dogmatic or practical.

Q.   *How do we do that?*
A.   In coming here, for example, some of you are beginning to understand that the rigid ideas you held about 'this is how it is' have been a limitation. You're beginning to realize that none of the information you accumulated over your lifetime held any truth about who you are.

This means that the information or seeming wisdom you first came here with is showing itself to be faulty. If all the concepts you hold about yourself are one day realized to be invalid, then the mind may give up trying to understand 'you.'

When the mind totally gives up trying to understand and realizes, 'I can never know the Truth,' in that instant Seeing happens beyond concepts.

Q.   *Enlightenment.*
A.   Relatively speaking light has been shed on the pseudo-identity, the personal lie. All the information you had about yourself is realized as false. You realize that You are not this accumulation of identities and that, essentially, there is no difference between 'you' and 'others.' In Reality there are no 'others.'

This means that the concept of guilt is unfounded. So guilt falls away too, and of course it is guilt that kept the 'me' desiring to become. Guilt underlies the whole struggle.

Once your blameless nature is 'remembered' the experiencing of manifestation continues unfolding from the stand-point of innocence. But it isn't the naïve innocence of the tiny child.

The mind is still full of information, but You know it doesn't hold any truth about You. This is true wisdom, the total conviction that the mind understands nothing about the Truth.

The 'process of enlightenment' relates to the stages of the naïvete of innocence, the accumulation of information and the realization that no information holds any Truth about who You are. You could call this the wisdom of innocence.

The 'wisdom of innocence' isn't naïve because it contains learned judgments and they don't all fall away—not imme-diately, and in some cases only partially, or very gradually.

Q. *I thought all judgments fell away?*
A. While there is a body, the mind still has to discriminate and make decisions. There is a difference between judging maliciously or with a personal agenda and making practical judgments. And do understand, the sage doesn't only make practical judgments. If the mind was fairly dogmatic preced-ing 'awakening,' some rigid judgments may continue.

Q. *But that sounds contradictory to everything you've been saying.*
A. Well, perhaps it sounds contradictory to what you have understood.

Q. *Yes, maybe that's it (laughing).*
A. While individuality is still strong, it's colored by the accu-mulation of information that preceded 'awakening.' Words that come out of the sage's mouth aren't necessarily correct and can even be so heavily colored by programming that they are quite off target. This can be the case, even though the sage Knows better.

Q. *But it's nice to think that the guru isn't going to confuse us further.*

A.   Yes, it's nice, but don't take anything any-one says on face value. That isn't to say that you should sit in front of the guru comparing your beliefs and agendas to what is being said.

If the guru's words go straight to your heart and an understanding happens that you can't put into words, don't even try. The mind has got out of the way and that in, and of, itself is enough. Then being in the presence of the guru was probably all that was necessary.

But there are lots of so-called gurus out there who are in the buddhi stage. They still have strong personalities and still have strong ideas. They can be wonderful teachers because they inspire you to look beyond your present rigid paradigm. But their paradigm is still not a total experiencing. They still have one foot in theory and can tend to teach primarily from this theory.

Q.   *Would you say you still teach from theory at all?*

A.   When I talk about the Absolute I am talking from the perspective of a deeply intuited understanding. I know that I Am not separate from That. I know I am That. But there is no direct awareness of It. So talking happens from this deeply intuited understanding only.

That I Am the impersonal functioning of Totality, expressing its-Self in manifestation is now the experiential state. It's not just an intellectual understanding. It's not a theory.

Until the phenomenon of duality is transcended there is no direct 'awareness' of the noumenon or non-dual (Absolute).

Even when it is a direct 'awareness,' it still can't be put into words. Of course, even to talk of 'direct awareness' can give the idea that some-one is aware of some-thing. Words really get in the way and to talk about it is to put concepts to That which is totally beyond concepts.

There is still a uniqueness of expression happening through

232

this body. This is the individuality, the love to be. Until this subsides whatever is said is, to some degree, colored by the unique expression of this intellect.

Only the words of the Sat-guru, such as Nisargadatta Maharaj, are relatively uncolored and more direct. Although the Truth can't be put into words, the Sat-guru's words point more directly to the Truth.

Simply being in the presence of the Sat-guru would be enough, if the 'understanding' was already very deep.

Q.   *You said I Am is now an experiential state. I thought you said that Self-realization is not a state?*
A.   That's true, but what I was meaning is that there is no-one, no pseudo-identity, experiencing a so-called 'state of consciousness.'

The experiencing of Self or manifest-Consciousness is only possible because there is a body through which it can happen. There is no Self, and no-one to experience it. There is only impersonal Experiencing happening via the body. This is registered by the intellect, although the intellect doesn't understand what has 'happened.'

What I'm referring to is the relative state of the bodymind *in-relation* to beingness.

The Knowing embodied in 'Esther' has nothing to do with that label. I Know I am not any label and that I'm not the body. But, beingness is experienced in a unique way through this physical mechanism.

Q.   *You still see the way it happens as unique to you then?*
A.   I see the impersonal functioning of Consciousness as happening in a unique way through this body. I know that who I Am is not the sum of this unique expression. I Know that I am not the sum of this individuality.

All there is Is Consciousness, expressing itself in various ways through various bodies. I Know that I am That which is beyond manifest expression, but is now experiencing its-

Self in the functioning of totality. But there is still orientation to the unique expression happening through this particular body.

Q. *But you don't experience other people's way of expressing in your body?*

A. No. Can you imagine that? What an overload. Actually in Vedantic teachings there is a 'stage' that is sometimes experienced called *mahat*. In mahat the universal Consciousness is experienced deeply. It's a pretty traumatic stage.

The second time I returned from seeing Ramesh I had a glimpse of this. For a few months I found it easier just to stay in seclusion. I'd go out and be around laughing children and seemingly happy parents and all I could feel was tremendous grief. I knew it wasn't 'my' grief, although it may have been a reflection of a holding in my own body.

Anyway, I wrote to Wendall and asked him to explain what I was experiencing. He wrote back saying, "What you are probably experiencing is the grief that is there when the Atman is not realized."

Q. *So it could have been your own grief then?*

A. Well, the 'me' had not totally dissolved, so yes it was probably grief still 'held' in this body. But it helped me understand that the pain of feeling separate is there even when people are apparently happy. I guess it gave me an understanding of just how well people cope.

Q. *Now you don't feel that pain anymore though?*

A. No. Now the mind still registers relative differences between expression through my body and that of 'others.' But it's clear that there is no real difference because no real 'others' exist. So there is no sense of separateness and no pain.

Appearances and relative differences—between these appearances—is recognized, that's all. I know that essen-

234

tially there are not-two. There is no separate 'other.'

Q. *Your perspective is still limited to your body though? You still experience everything from the perspective of your body?*

A. Without a body could you experience being?

Q. *I don't know.*

A. Do you remember ever not having the experience of being? Will you ever know the experience of not being?

Q. *No.*

A. Before the body, and after the body, you have no idea of what happened, or will happen, to this beingness, isn't that so?

Q. *Yes.*

A. When you close your eyes and experience simply being conscious you discover that this sense has no location and isn't limited to, or by, the body. Isn't that so?

Q. *Yes.*

A. Well, where do you think this consciousness could go if the body wasn't there?

Q. *Nowhere.*

A. If it can go nowhere how do you think it could come from somewhere?

Q. *I guess it couldn't.*

A. This means that it has never not existed, and that it can never end. Do you see that?

Q. *Yes.*

A. Consciousness is all there Is. Things, bodies, appear to be 'born,' change, move to other locations, and die. This is all a spontaneous happening within Consciousness, which has never been born and never dies.

When the body appears, the idea of some-one 'being

235

conscious' arises. Has that changed Consciousness in any way do you think?

Q.   *No.*

A.   In this case that idea has subsided. When Consciousness first expressed its-Self via this body in relation to other bodies, the love of being began to grow. Now even this love of being is waning.

In some cases, while the body exists, this dispassion becomes total. In others, it is dispelled only gradually or very slightly. In some cases, such as Nisargadatta Maharaj, the body becomes diseased and the pain unbearable. This pain can seem to accelerate dispassion for the beingness. In the case of Shankara of the North, this 'happened' while the body was healthy and his body still lives on.

When individuality dissolves to but a trace, then Self-consciousness and duality are 'transcended.' Nisargadatta Maharaj points to this Transcendent-Consciousness as 'awareness of awareness,' but clearly no words exist to describe or explain That which is beyond concepts.

Q.   *So you experience the Self, but have not transcended it?*

A.   Yes. But do understand that there is no experiencer and no Self to be experienced. There is Experiencing minus labels. Because there is not total dispassion towards this Experiencing (manifest-Consciousness) it has not been 'transcended.' But I am not saying that there is any-one to transcend any-thing.

The word transcended is perhaps confusing. Maybe it's clearer to say that when the 'I' individuality, or love of being neutralizes to but a trace, I Am-consciousness, the body, mind and all of duality subside into the Absolute. But do understand that manifest-Self and the Absolute in which it arises are not-two.

Perhaps one could explain the myth of creation this way: Within the Absolute the appearance of manifestation unfolds. This is a spontaneous happening and doesn't have anything to do with a 'decision' the Absolute makes.

Q.   *You mean it's not like there's a higher power who decides to cause creation?*
A.   If you were God, do you think you'd voluntarily decide, "Ah, I think I'll create a world full of pain and suffering so I can experience limitation?"

Q.   *No.*
A.   People like the theory of creation and the idea of God. The trouble is they can't understand why there is pain and suffering. The only way of reconciling with it is by coming up with the idea of a Devil who does all the bad stuff. Then, of course, when they are having a hard time the Devil can be blamed. When they are doing something they think is bad it means they are under the power of the Devil.

It's a pretty self-defeating theory really, but religions thrive on it. It means their followers will keep on coming back for dispensation. After all, the heads of religions have a direct line to God. Heck, there are even TV programs where you can phone in and talk to God via His chosen ones.

Q.   *Yes, that's so weird.*
A.   Yes. The dichotomy between God, the Devil, heaven and hell, is really symbolic of the 'split' mind. Those concepts give vivid imagery to the unhealthy ego's battle with good and evil. The emotional swings between the internal heaven and hell. It's much easier to project it all outwards.

Q.   *I guess.*
A.   This world appearance isn't lauded over by higher powers. Duality is a spontaneous unfolding within the Absolute— neutrality. Via duality, Consciousness is aware of its-Self. Via the body, the love of being happens and the cause of this experience is then attributed to the body.

With this misperception comes the experience of limitation. Self-love then wanes, but the love of being usually persists.

This gives rise to the idea that what is limited and seems lacking can be improved upon.

Self-love is replaced by the quest for self-gratification. When all improvements and desires to 'become' are unfulfilled, the mind turns gradually away from the objective world. If this in-turning is strong enough, manifest-Consciousness, 'I Am,' the body and mind and all of duality subsides in the Absolute.

The body is necessary for both the no-knowing of Self and Knowing to 'happen.'

But the Absolute, from which Self has never been separate, is unaffected by this 'dependency.' The Absolute is beyond no-knowingness and Knowing. It is the Ultimate Knowledge —often called 'the highest state.' Again, that 'state' simply refers to the embodiment of this 'Knowledge' in the Sat-guru.

Consciousness expressing its-Self in the innocence of the tiny child is easily distracted. Similarly, when the wisdom of innocence 'happens,' Consciousness once again becomes distracted. It is distracted from this beingness, and the love to be and dispassion, or neutrality, deepens.

One could say that the 'neutralizing' of Self-consciousness is necessary before subsidence into the Absolute neutrality 'happens.' The term Sat-guru describes the embodiment of Transcendent-Consciousness.

It's just a story, but one that you now experience having a personal part in. No higher power or intelligence decided upon this story—it is a spontaneous unfolding within the Absolute.

You didn't decide to take a personal part in it, nor can you voluntarily stop playing the part that you consider 'you.' But perhaps all this will give you a clearer perspective on where 'you' are at in this story.

Until the myth is recognized for what it is, these are just

words that point away from your present experience. These words are filtered through this particular intellect and so colored by it. But they may help distract you from the personal lie you think of as 'me.' These words may have the benefit of intensifying your own investigation. And that is all that's necessary—that there is an intensity to know the Truth.

There has to be an all-consuming intensity to see beyond the labels and concepts. When this yearning catches fire it consumes all other desires and 'your head is in the Tiger's mouth' as they say. The 'you' who feels this intensity begins being consumed by this 'fire.' Then it doesn't matter what you do or don't do. Nothing you do is going to accelerate this process.

If these words, or simply being here, triggers an 'understanding' that you can't put into words, then don't even try. When tears fall and questions temporarily subside, it means the words have bypassed your mind. The heart has 'absorbed' what is being communicated. Then let what happens just happen and don't try to understand it.

If you feel the need to do something, focus on this beingness (I Am). Then there is only one question to ask—how do you know that you are?

The Divine is reflected in the love of being.
When 'I Am' is free of labels the Knowing is there that
You and the Divine are not-two. This can only happen
when the mind ceases censoring the heart.
To realize the Divine within your own heart is to See its
reflection everywhere, in everything. This reflection and the
Seeing of it is dependent on the Eternal principle in
which they appear, and You are That.

un-learn